THE NEW!
IMPROVED!
Bob & Ray
BOOK

Bob Elliott and Ray Goulding

FOREWORD BY GARRISON KEILLOR

G. P. PUTNAM'S SONS / NEW YORK

G. P. Putnam's Sons
Publishers Since 1838
200 Madison Avenue
New York, NY 10016

Library of Congress Cataloging in Publication Data

Elliott, Bob.
The new! improved! Bob and Ray book.

Includes index.
1. American wit and humor.   I. Goulding, Ray.
II. Title.
PN6162.E43   1985   818'.5407   85-6287
ISBN 0-399-13085-3

Printed in the United States of America
1   2   3   4   5   6   7   8   9   10

Contents

Foreword

BY GARRISON KEILLOR

As a loyal Bob & Ray fan, I've often imagined what it would be like to meet them in person and to sit around and josh, perhaps in my own home or else in the coffeeshop on the mezzanine of the Bob & Ray Building. In my loyal fan heart, I naturally assume we'll hit it off big from the start. In fact, I imagine Bob picking me out of a crowd of fans clustered around him and his partner at a Gotham autograph party where they are patiently enduring a lot of admiration and signing "Bob" and "Ray" in thousands of their latest books. His face brightens when he sees me. "The tall one with the glasses!" he calls out. "Let that man through!" Other fans resent this. "Hey, we've been here since late this *morning!*" they mutter as I edge forward apologetically but forcefully and take his outstretched hand. "I don't know, I just sensed an affinity there," he says. "Hi, pal," says Ray. "Come over to our coffeeshop and let's hobnob."

Meeting our favorite celebrities: we all imagine what it would be like and spend a little time now and then rehearsing for the event, often while driving to work. Sometimes at an intersection, I notice other drivers suddenly brighten and plunge into witty conversation with their windshields, and I guess they are probably charming the pants off an illustrious person on an experimental basis. I myself, though I have run through some dialogue with Meryl Streep, never practice conversing with Bob and Ray because I want that first meeting to be a fresh experience, not something I know by heart.

In the coffeeshop, of course, I don't start off by quoting dozens of their funniest lines or doing the voices of theirs that I do fairly

well, such as Aunt Penny, Dean Archer Armstead, and Wally
Ballou. I've seen fans who come on strong like that, and invari-
ably the famous person says, "Hey, catch you later." So, as we sit
down around a linoleum-topped table with the familiar B&R
logo and order coffee, I am being pretty calm, not trying to score
points, listening, smiling, waiting for an opening—a chance re-
mark of Ray's perhaps, inquiring as to my occupation. I say, "I'm
in lead mining. It's something that's in my blood, I guess. Lead, I
mean." And suddenly his solemn demeanor is convulsed by
laughter—Bob laughs too, and his big blue eyes dart across the
table and back. "There's a place in our organization for a person
of your caliber," he says. "You name it," Ray chuckles.

Of course, every fan's dream is a chance to join the Bobaloos or
the Rayons, the crack big band and vocal ensemble who fly with
Bob & Ray to their personal appearances on the coast. These
wonderful guys and gals also appear in comedy spots, providing
crowd hubbub, scream, running footsteps, sirens, gunshots, creak-
ing masts on schooners, whinnies and horses' hooves, landslides,
clinking glasses, and footsteps on polished parquet floors. They do
all these with only their mouths, their fingernails and a No. 2
pencil. Plus they play instruments and/or sing. But the life of a
Rayon or a Bobaloo is not for me, I'm afraid—I just have too
much anger bottled up inside me to ever make the wonderful
music they make—I guess the part of the Bob & Ray team I fit is
the law enforcement arm.

All the years these fine gentlemen have been entertaining us via
radio, various individuals have faithfully recorded their stuff and
(this is the part that gripes me) made copies of the stuff and sold
them. In Seattle, Los Angeles, Atlanta, Manhattan, I've seen Bob
& Ray tapes sold that, due to the childlike artwork and lack of
corporate name and address, appeared to be bootleg copies from
which, thanks to modern electronics, the writers get not a penny.

Let me give you guys some advice: don't *ever* cheat a writer,
don't even *think* about it. When you cheat Bob & Ray, then you
have crossed the line that separates you from me and my viselike
grip. I'm white, approximately seven feet tall, and wear black
clothing. I have good lateral movement. If you have sold Bob &
Ray material feloniously, look out. I am watching from across the
street as you chuckle over this book, and I am squeezing a regula-

tion softball in my left hand. When I finish the Lucky, I'll be suddenly in the room with you, and you'll be reading in the dim light of my immense shadow. I want a check from you for twelve percent of the gross, made out to Bob & Ray, which you can start writing now while your hand is steady, and unless you ate Dumb Flakes for breakfast, you'll want to be sure that the check is one of the best you ever wrote.

FEATURING

Wally Ballou   Edna Bessinger   Biff Burns

Word Wizard Elmer Stapley   Big Steve Wurbler

Gordon Offenhouser   Chalmers Boatwright   Winona Fifer

J. P. Warmerdam of the Merchants United Eastern
First Federal Manhattan Security Trust Company

Holden Merkly   Hoyt Netley   Agatha Murchfield

Lloyd the gardener   Ralph Flinger   Ward Stuffer

The Right Honorable G. L. Hummerbeck   Farley Girard

Young Doctor Honeycutt   Old Doctor Gilroy

Berne Voyle   Neil Clummer   Mulford B. Thaxter

Fern Ock Veek, Sickly Whale Oil Processor

Vidal Sassoon (not him, another one)   Marco Polo (same here)

Officer Wishmiller of the Alaska State Highway Patrol

Merton Chesny   Herbert Botchford   Shifty Wayman

Godfrey Blandish   Shaky Dopflyer   Carlton E. Wickwire

Emil Ruppnicker   Claude Flabbert   Wilmont Shriber

Tippy, the Wonder Dog   Walter Kettlehut

Lupis Bartlow, Agatha Benchlow, Pamela Buntlow, Gordon Bozlow,
Tod Berklow *and* Walter Breaklow

BULLETIN

The Follansbee Nut Ranch in Kernel County urgently needs experienced walnut pickers to aid in harvesting the walnut crop which will reach maturity within the next twenty-four hours. If you have experience in picking walnuts, please contact Mr. Harvey Follansbee, Follansbee Nut Ranch, Kernel County, at once. Transportation, plus all the walnuts you can eat will be furnished, in addition to attractive wages.

Wally Ballou Interviews W-W-Q-L-C-W

BOB

Well, hi again, everybody, and welcome to another Bob and Ray show. This is Bob Elliott . . .

RAY

. . . and this is Ray Goulding, and we've got a whole lot in store for you today. Makes my skin tingle just thinking about it. But first I have word that correspondent Wally Ballou is standing by with what he tells us is one of the most unusual and interesting interviews he's ever lined up. So come in, please, Wally Ballou . . .

BALLOU

—ly Ballou standing with a gentleman my staff tells me is one of the most unusual and interesting interviews we've ever lined up. I wonder if you'd tell us your name, sir?

MAN

No, I'm afraid I can't do that . . .

BALLOU

You hiding from the police or something like that?

MAN

No. I can't tell you my name because I am one of the very few people in America with a name that is completely unpronounce-able.

BALLOU

Well . . . could you spell it for us?

MAN

That's all you can do with it. It's spelled: W-W-Q-L-C-W.

BALLOU

W-W-Q-L-C-W. Are you sure that's a name and not the call letters of some radio station?

MAN

No, it's my name all right. But there's no way to pronounce it. I've been trying for years, and it's got me beat.

BALLOU

I certainly never heard it before. What nationality is it?

MAN

Well, my grandfather came from Iraq, originally. And I've got a hunch that when he changed the letters from the Arabic alphabet into English, he goofed something awful.

BALLOU

I guess that could be. Do you still have relatives back in the old country?

MAN

Oh yeah. Cousins . . . and things like that.

Courtesy of Hartford Insurance Company

BALLOU

How do they pronounce the name?

MAN

They pronounce it Abernathy.

BALLOU

Well, I don't see how you possibly could get Abernathy out of that jumble of letters you rattled off!

MAN

No, I don't either. That's what made me think Grandpa really loused up the translation when he got here.

BALLOU

I should think having a name like yours would create quite a few problems for you.

MAN

Yes, it does. Like, the phone company refuses to list me in the directory. When I spelled the name for them, they thought I was some kind of nut.

BALLOU

I can see how they would.

MAN

And you take like when my home was robbed . . . they ran a little story in our local paper about it. And the linotype operator got fired.

BALLOU

How come?

MAN

Well, my name was mentioned three times in the story. And the publisher figured that anybody who'd make that many typographical errors in one paragraph must be drunk!

BALLOU

Too bad the fellow lost his job because of your name.

MAN

I felt terrible. I wanted to call the publisher, but I couldn't because I didn't know how to pronounce who I was.

BALLOU

What do you do in your everyday life? Go by your first name?

MAN

I don't have one. You see, my folks didn't know what would go well with our last name because they never figured out how to pronounce it. So my birth certificate just lists me as Infant W-W-Q-L-C-W . . .

BALLOU

I see.

MAN

But I think it would be ridiculous for a forty-seven-year-old man to go around calling himself Infant!

BALLOU

I agree. And now this is Wally Ballou saying thanks and so long until next time . . .

MAN

I'd like to say hello to my brother on your program, but I don't know how to pronounce his name either!

The Word Wizard

BOB

And now it's time for another informative session with Doctor Elmer Stapley, the Word Wizard. Doctor Stapley is one of the nation's leading authorities on the meaning and derivation of English words. And he's here to answer the questions that you listeners send in about our language and its correct use. Doctor, we didn't have time to go over the mail in advance this week. So I hope you won't be thrown by any of the questions.

STAPLEY

Mr. Elliott—that last statement of yours is so puncturized that it's almost hypocritical. You see, a question is not only an intangible object—it's also dead. Thereby, it's possible to be thrown by a horse or any simulated form of human life that's an animal. But it's psychogenically impossible to be thrown by a question. Do I make myself conspicuous?

BOB

Yes—but then, you always do. So it's really our fault for inviting you back. And all we can do now is hope that you won't be thrown by any of this week's questions. Our first letter to the Word Wizard comes from a woman in Ohio. She writes: "I am very upset about the grammar my nine-year-old son uses. Every day, he comes home and says, 'I ain't gotten no money.' How can I explain this complicated mistake so he'll stop saying it?"

STAPLEY

Well, I don't see what's complicated. Just tell him to get a job and earn some money. Then he'll stop saying he doesn't have any.

BOB

Well, I don't think that quite answers the woman's question, Doctor. Her son is only nine, so he can't very well get a job. I think she just wants to explain to him why it's wrong to say, "I ain't gotten no money."

STAPLEY

Well, problematically, the thing that's bothering her is that word "gotten." You see, her son is using the past icicle instead of the present tension. But that's hard to explain to a child. So I'd suggest having the kid use a completely different verbal and say, "I ain't in possession of no money."

BOB

And that's the only grammatical change in the sentence you'd recommend?!

STAPLEY

Of course. And please don't try to change my mind—because once I've solved a problem, I remain abominable.

BOB

Well, I know you've always seemed that way to me. But I thought maybe I was just prejudiced. However, I guess we've taken care of the woman's question, and can move on to another one . . . This next letter comes from a man in California. He writes: "I bought a lot of soft drinks that had the words 'No Deposit—No Return' printed on the bottles. I tried to obey my part of the instructions by not paying any deposit when I bought them. But now—when I try to take back the empties—the clerk returns them to me, even though they say 'No Return.' Is there something about the way the instructions are phrased that I've misunderstood?''

STAPLEY

What were those words again that he wanted me to interrogate?

BOB

No deposit—no return.

STAPLEY

Well, that doesn't make sense. It's not even a complete sentence.

BOB

No, it isn't. But, of course, this man lives in California. And they print a lot of ungrammatical things on their bottles out there. So I think we can just skip the question and move on to another one here. . . . This last letter comes from a lady in North Carolina. And she writes: "I work on the switchboard for a firm called Fleckny, Ignass, Wateford and Swope. Frequently, I get calls from people who want to talk to Mr. Fleckny, Mr. Ignass, Mr. Wateford or Mr. Swope. If they're all out to lunch, should I say, 'None of them is here' or 'None of them are here'?''

STAPLEY

Well, first, I think she should look around to make sure they're gone. It's pretty unusual for all of the top people in a company to go out to lunch at the same time.

BOB

Well, apparently they do go at the same time in this firm. Otherwise the woman wouldn't need to know whether to say "None of them is here" or "None of them are here."

STAPLEY

Well, it strikes me as a heck of a way to run a business. But viewing it strictly as a grammatician, the correct thing to say is: "All of them are not around."

BOB

Yes. I'm sure that would get the message across. So I'm sure you've solved this lady's problem—and also helped our other ignorant listeners. And I want to thank you for being with us today, Doctor.

STAPLEY

Not at all. I was petrified to come.

BOB

Well, we always get a little nervous about having you here, too. But we seem to keep inviting you back anyway. So I guess we'll be seeing you again soon on another of these informative sessions with—Doctor Elmer Stapley, the Word Wizard.

The Gathering Dusk

(*Theme: "Stardust." Establish and under for*)

BOB

And now the Auburn Motor Company—maker of fine cars up to but not including 1938—brings you another episode of *The Gathering Dusk*—the heartwarming story of a girl who hides behind a shield of indecision because it's the safest place to hide.
(*Theme up briefly and then fade for*)

BOB

As we look in on the Bessinger household today, Edna is pondering the meaning of life in the downstairs cupboard. It is late afternoon—and Doctor Engelbretzen, the chief endocrinologist at the small clinic in the village, is just arriving.
(*Footsteps*)

EDNA

Oh, it's you, Small Village Clinic Endocrinologist Engelbretzen. It was kind of you to answer my urgent call so quickly. I hope you weren't busy pumping some child full of serum to turn him into an eight-foot basketball player.

ENGELBRETZEN

No. Certainly not, Miss Bessinger. An endocrinologist never tampers with the body chemistry if it's functioning properly.

EDNA

Well, I'm awfully glad to hear that you people have adopted a more humane policy like that. I remember years ago when doctors forced all kinds of pills down my brother Waldo. They tried to change his whole personality.

ENGELBRETZEN

Well, that was a little different, Miss Bessinger. They had him in the prison hospital because he was a homicidal maniac.

EDNA

Well, that seems like a pretty strong term to use. I admit that Waldo was an impetuous boy. But I'm sure he would have outgrown being so hot-headed if people had just left him alone.

ENGELBRETZEN

Well, as I recall, he'd already shot up the town three or four times. So I guess the police decided they couldn't wait any longer for him to outgrow his problem.

EDNA

I suppose that's true. But of course, Waldo never struck without provocation. It wasn't until he'd been turned down for the small loan that he blew up the bank.

ENGELBRETZEN

Yes. Well, that's the type of reaction that would be considered abnormal.

EDNA

Well, I think Old Banker Mosely's reaction was the one that was abnormal. Waldo certainly had good collateral for the loan. He was holding Mrs. Mosely hostage. And all he wanted in exchange for her life was two hundred dollars.

ENGELBRETZEN

Miss Bessinger—all that type of thing went against your brother before he was sent away for treatment. I saw the report of the court-appointed psychiatrists. And they all concurred that he wasn't playing with a full deck.

EDNA

That's just a clinical term. And you would have had to know Waldo to appreciate what a good boy he was. He even took care of the Moselys' dog free of charge after the whole family passed away.

ENGELBRETZEN

I know. But he was also responsible for making the whole family pass away. However, I don't imagine you called me over here just to discuss reopening your brother's case after all these years.

EDNA

No. You're right as rain about that, Small Village Clinic Endocrinologist Engelbretzen. I've just been in a terrible snit today because one of my glands has gone completely haywire. I was barely five feet tall when I got up this morning. And look at me now. I keep bumping my head on the light fixtures when I walk around. If I don't stop growing soon, I just don't know what I'm going to do.

ENGELBRETZEN

Well, I'm sure I see what your problem is, Miss Bessinger. But it has nothing to do with your endocrine system. You've been standing on a pair of stilts ever since I got here.

EDNA

Glory be! So I have. And I'll bet a nickel that's what's added several feet to my height. I found these stilts up in the attic this morning while I was rummaging through some of my childhood treasures. And I had so much fun trying them on again that I completely forgot I still had them on. My! You can't imagine what a terrible worry this lifts from my mind, Small Village Clinic Endocrinologist Engelbretzen. Why, I almost feel as if I'm no longer standing in . . . The Gathering Dusk.

(Theme up briefly and then out)

BULLETIN

Following the earlier announcement that the Follansbee Nut Ranch in Kernel County needed experienced walnut pickers at once, we wish to advise prospective pickers that while transportation to the ranch will be furnished, this does not include airplane travel. And remember: contact Mrs. Harvey Follansbee . . . not Mr. Harvey Follansbee.

You and Your Symptoms

BOB

More valuable health tips, as we present *You and Your Symptoms*. Back with us to answer the questions you listeners send in is one of the nation's top medical authorities, Dr. L. L. Barnstall. I assume, sir, that the backlog of malpractice charges you were facing has been cleared away and that it's all right to call you "doctor" again.

BARNSTALL

Well, my professional status in this country is still pretty shaky. But I slipped ten bucks to the Katanga government in exile, and they issued me a license to do whatever I please with no questions asked.

BOB

Well, I'm sure that will install our afflicted listeners' confidence, so let's take up this first letter from a woman in Minnesota. She writes: "I seem to be normal and healthy in every way, except for the fact that I have leaves growing out of my head in place of hair. I don't mind it too much in the spring and summer. But in autumn, I know I'll start to shed—and the job of raking up the house three or four times a day is a terrible nuisance. Can anything be done to alleviate my condition?"

BARNSTALL

Actually, this is more a problem for a tree surgeon than for whatever it is I happen to be. However, I would assume that the trouble starts when the frost causes the sap to drain out of the woman's head. So lighting smudge pots around her roots should prevent—

BOB

Excuse me, Doctor—but this woman is not entirely a tree. She just has leaves growing out of her head.

BARNSTALL

Oh, well, in that case, she probably isn't even susceptible to the chestnut blight and I'm sure there's no cause for alarm. The leaves should sprout again next spring and, with luck, her head may even blossom. What's next?

BOB

Well, I have one here—

BARNSTALL

Some people imagine the worst when they have the slightest symptom and go running to a doctor. They think doctors can work miracles.

BOB

Yes. Well, listening to your advice should cure them of that. Now I have a letter here from a man in Arizona. He writes: "I have often regretted the fact that I dropped out of medical school before I finished. Now I'm almost forty. Do you think I'm too old to go back and complete my studies?"

BARNSTALL

A man never becomes too old to prepare himself for the noble practice of medicine. The desire to become a doctor and alleviate the suffering of the afflicted knows no age limit. For who is to say when, in the course of our lives, the burning ambition to serve humanity may strike—and lead us to shout from the rooftops, "I shall—I must become a doctor"?

BOB

Gee, that was inspiring. Did one of your professors at medical school say that?

BARNSTALL

Maybe. I can't be sure. I dropped out before I finished.

BOB

I see. Well, then, suppose we move along to this next letter from a woman in Illinois. She writes: "Recently, I had a medical checkup in an effort to find out why I keep gaining weight. Afterward, my doctor told me that my hemoglobin was not overly dilapidory on the Richter scale—my cholesterol count was not endangering a cardiac malfunction—and that my metabolism rate merely indicated an abnormal caloric intake in proportion to my physical activity output in British thermal units. What do you think this means?"

BARNSTALL

I think it means she goes to a doctor who only speaks Spanish.

BOB

Okay. Well, that should relieve her mind. And I think we have time for just one more quickie here from a man in Utah. He writes: "Are you the same L. L. Barnstall who charged me for taking out my appendix in 1981? And if so, how do you explain the fact that recent X rays showed I still have an appendix plus a sponge and a pair of scissors inside—but no digestive system?"

BARNSTALL

Well, any discussion with a layman concerning the human anatomy tends to—I mean, once in a while when you're in there rummaging around, you uhh— And besides, I think I just heard an ambulance siren, which probably means I'm urgently needed someplace. Good-bye.
(Hurried footsteps and door slam)

BOB

And so the doctor takes his hurried leave on another errand of mercy. But be sure to join us next time when he'll be wandering back with more valuable health tips on *You and Your Symptoms.*

Biff Burns's Sports Room

BURNS

This is Biff Burns coming your way from mikeside for another long look at the highlights and sidelights from the world of sports. My special guest here in the sports room is Big Steve Wurbler . . . a name I'm sure you'll be hearing a lot more often because he's the world champion high jumper. Welcome to the sports room, Big Steve.

WURBLER

Thanks very much, Biff. Incidentally, you made one little mistake there that I'd like to correct. You said that I'm the world champion high jumper. Actually, I'm the champion low jumper.

BURNS

Well, I'm sure there's very little difference between the two events. What's your best mark in the low jump, Big Steve?

WURBLER

I've jumped 57 feet 8 inches, Biff. That's about 50 feet farther than the world record in the high jump.

BURNS

Well, it sounds as if there may be more than a little difference between the two events, then, Big Steve. And, of course, you and I know what that difference is. But I wonder if you'd explain it to the fans at home?

WURBLER

Yeah, sure. I'd be happy to. You see . . . in high jumping you stand in a low place and see how far up you can jump. And in low jumping, you stand on a high place and see how far down you can jump.

BURNS

I see. Well, of course, you and I both know the answer to this next question, Big Steve. But for the benefit of the fans listening in, I wonder if you'd comment on whether that's all there is to it?

WURBLER

Well, basically, yes. I might just add that if you jump down from a high place and get killed, then the jump doesn't count. That's why my 57 feet 8 inches still stands as an all-time record.

BURNS

I hate to come right out and ask what might be an embarrassing question for you, Big Steve. But isn't this kind of a dumb sport that would only appeal to a big lummox like yourself, who has rocks in his head?

WURBLER

Well, yeah. I guess you could make a good argument for that point, Biff. But, personally, I think low jumping's got it all over high jumping. I mean, in high jumping, you can strain a muscle or hurt yourself on the way up—or you can break some bones when you fall on the way down. But in low jumping, you only have to worry about what happens to you on the way down.

BURNS

Yes, I can see the logic there. Even if it may be a little too compli-cated for some of the fans to understand. But in any event, I hear that you're now trying to get low jumping recognized as a major track and field event . . . and to have it included in the Olympics.

WURBLER

To be truthful, so far we haven't been too successful in getting the Olympics people fired up. There's a private promoter here in New York who's willing to rent a spot on the Palisades and have us all jump into the Hudson River. But, of course, it's not an official low jump when you land in water or anything soft like that.

BURNS

Oh? I thought the only object was to live through the event. I didn't know the surface you landed on made a difference, too.

WURBLER

Oh, yeah. I jump mostly onto concrete or asphalt. But you can also jump onto natural ground . . . providing it hasn't been softened by rain, or any other type of moisture.

BURNS

What about Astro-turf and things like that?

WURBLER

Yes. Astro-turf is okay—if the grass is not long enough to break your fall. Of course, it can't be softened by moisture, either.

BURNS

Well, I can see that the rules are fairly strict on that. So, if low jumping should be recognized as an Olympic sport, I guess you'll have to do it someplace—like from the window of an office building?

WURBLER

Yeah, we could. But that's not the best arrangement, either. In case of a tie, you'd have to move up one whole floor at a time . . .

which is about 10 feet. So, I'd favor having the guys jump off a fire department ladder or something like that, where you can go up just a little at a time.

BURNS

I see. And about how many entries do you think there'll be from around the world in a low jumping event?

WURBLER

Well, Biff . . . judging from the mail I've received . . . I think there'd be two. One is a Tibetan who puts himself into a trance and jumps off mountains. And the other is a guy in France who seems pretty flaky, too.

BURNS

Okay. So there'd be those two. And then, counting yourself, the total number of entries would be three?

WURBLER

No, I've decided not to compete, Biff. I think it would take a real fruitcake to try to beat the 57-foot record I already hold. And, also, I know from experience that low jumping more than 30 or 40 feet gives you a terrible headache. So, I say . . . who needs it?

BURNS

That's what I was tempted to say as soon as you started talking about the sport, Big Steve. But now you've said it for me. Thanks for dropping by the sports room for this story . . . and this is Biff Burns saying until next time . . . this is Biff Burns saying . . . so long fans!

Hard Luck Stories

(Organ: Sad theme in and establish and under for)

RAY

Next—more Hard Luck Stories. We've had our scouts searching the railroad and bus stations here for victims of misfortune who need a helping hand from our generous Bob and Ray Organization . . .

BOB

We like to have them pour out their misery here on the show, and here's our first crestfallen figure, Mr. Stanley Waldrop, of Duluth, Minnesota. . . . And, Mr. Waldrop, I understand that you've just spent your life savings on a futile trip halfway around the world to hunt for your missing sister.

WALDROP

That's right, Bob and Ray. I hunted all over Roumania for her. But it was just a year of my life wasted.

BOB

Well, that is indeed tragic, Mr. Waldrop. And I assume your search centered on Roumania because that's where your family came from.

WALDROP

No. We've lived in Minnesota for generations. But when I was a little kid, my friend next door had a baby sister. So I asked my folks why I couldn't have one, too. And they kept saying I already had a sister—but she was carried off by gypsies.

BOB

I see. And so you decided to hunt for her in Roumania because that's where most of the gypsy tribes live. Is that it?

WALDROP

Yeah. That's right. I went from one gypsy camp to another. But I couldn't find anybody who'd seen my sister. So I finally came home.

BOB

You just got discouraged and gave up, eh?

WALDROP

No. I didn't get discouraged exactly. But when I told my story to one gypsy over there, he expressed the opinion that I probably never had a sister—and my parents just lied to me so I'd stop bugging them. That sounded reasonable—so I came home.

BOB

Well, we know how difficult it must have been for you to face the obvious, Mr. Waldrop. But to ease your sorrow, our generous Bob and Ray Organization wants you to have this sturdy new anchor for your yacht. It's from the Sand and Surf Iron Foundry of Miami, Florida.

WALDROP

Well, I don't have a yacht. In fact, I could barely afford a ticket home on a tramp steamer.

BOB

Don't try to thank me, sir. Just use it in good health. . . . Now with today's next Hard Luck Story, here is Mrs. Bessie Wilmerding of Rolla, Missouri. And—

WILMERDING

Excuse me, but that's not Mrs. Wilmerding. It's Doctor Wilmerding. I'm an anthropologist.

BOB

Oh, I'm sorry, Doctor. I should have guessed you were a Ph.D. from your card here. It says you're leading an expedition to search for a primitive tribe that's still living in the Stone Age.

WILMERDING

Yes. Hunting for lost tribes like that is all the rage with anthropologists now. But there don't seem to be any left in New Guinea or the Philippines that haven't been discovered yet. So I'm using my own savings to hunt for one in New York.

BOB

You expect to find a tribe here that still has a Stone Age culture?!

WILMERDING

Yes. My brother-in-law was here about a year ago. And he said he ran into some people out in Queens who seemed awfully crude to him. But I haven't found any trace of them yet.

BOB

Well, it must be heartbreaking to get this close to a great discovery—and then have all the natives go into hiding. But our generous Bob and Ray Organization wants to reward you for your efforts with this lovely pair of oversize foam rubber dice. See how they're tied together so they can be hung conveniently from the rearview mirror of your car?

WILMERDING

Well, I don't want anything like that to be seen in my car. I have a doctoral degree in anthropology.

BOB

You're entirely welcome. We knew you'd appreciate the thought. . . . Now, with today's final Hard Luck Story, here is Mr. Ozzie Wheelwright of Bedford, Indiana. And, sir, I understand you spent your life savings on a trip to New York in the hope of advancing your professional career.

WHEELWRIGHT

That's right. I make wax grapes for fruit markets to put on display so customers can't ruin the real grapes by squeezing them. And I thought New York would offer more opportunities than Bedford, Indiana. I've already sold wax grapes to all the stores back there—and they don't need to be replaced very often.

BOB

Well, there should be thousands of potential customers for you in New York. What went wrong?

WHEELWRIGHT

Well, New Yorkers seem to be a little more hotheaded than people in Bedford. Here, when they squeeze grapes and find out they're phony—they tend to throw the grapes at the store owners. And if you've ever been pelted with wax grapes all day, you know what a splitting headache it can give you.

BOB

Well, actually, I've never been pelted with wax grapes for any length of time. But I can appreciate how that would cause fruit store owners to turn against your product. However, our Bob and Ray Organization is going to help you get a new start in life with this valuable gift. It's a deluxe, electrically powered room air freshener. And it comes complete with batteries and two spray can refills.

WHEELWRIGHT

Gee, I don't know what to say. I figured my life was ruined—but this suddenly changes everything.

BOB

Don't try to thank me, sir. Just use it good health. And now, back over to Ray at our main anchor desk.
(*Organ: Sad theme up and end*)

Lupis Bartlow, Counselor-at-Law

(*Theme: "Pomp and Circumstance." Establish and under for*)

RAY

And now the Inter-Mountain Baby Food Cartel—the world's largest packager of mooshed-up vegetables for your little one—presents another session of courtroom drama starring . . . Lupis Bartlow, Counselor-at-Law.
(*Theme up full and then fade for*)

RAY

As our scene opens today, Lupis Bartlow appears to be losing his fight to gain acquittal for shy, demure Agatha Benchlow. Only the missing mystery witness who saw the shooting of Gordon Bozlow from a nearby apartment window can save Agatha now. But hope of finding that witness is all but gone—when suddenly Lupis Bartlow's young associate, Tod Berklow, comes bursting into the courtroom.
(*Running footsteps and crowd murmur*)

BARTLOW

(*Sotto*) So you've finally found her, Tod. Good work. With the testimony of this mystery witness, we'll punch holes in the case against Agatha Benchlow. (*Full voice*) Your honor, the defense calls to the stand Mrs. Pamela Buntlow.

OFFICER

Pamela Buntlow to the stand.
                    (*Footsteps and crowd murmur*)

BAILIFF

You swear (*mumble*) truth (*mumble*) so help you.

BUNTLOW

Yes. I do.

BARTLOW

Now, Mrs. Buntlow, I want you to remember as best you can the evening of last August 19th. Were you at home in your apartment?

BUNTLOW

Well, not all evening—no. I belong to a canasta club that meets on August 19th. So I wouldn't have gotten home until around eleven that night.

BARTLOW

The precise time of your arrival is most important, Mrs. Buntlow. Wasn't it really closer to 11:30?

PROSECUTION ATTORNEY

Objection. He's leading the witness.

JUDGE

Sustained.

PROSECUTION ATTORNEY

Gotcha that time, Bartlow.

BARTLOW

I'll rephrase the question, your honor. . . . Now, Mrs. Buntlow, try to think exactly what time you arrived at your apartment on August 19th.

BUNTLOW

Well, I do recall now that the eleven o'clock news was on the car radio as I left the girls. And driving home at that hour would have taken about twenty or twenty-five minutes. So I guess it must have been 11:30 by the time I got there.

BARTLOW

Very well. And would you now tell us—was there a great deal of gunfire and screaming in progress on the front steps of your building as you entered?

BUNTLOW

No. I'm sure there wasn't. I would have remembered that.

BARTLOW

Of course you would. That means the victim, Gordon Bozlow, was still alive at 11:30 P.M. Yet we have heard the testimony from the defendant's houseboy, Walter Breaklow, that he heard Agatha Benchlow arrive home at 11:15. And you're quite sure of the time you came in, Mrs. Buntlow?

BUNTLOW

Yes. It was 11:30—maybe even 11:35.

BARTLOW

Very good. Now would you be kind enough to tell the court how long you had been home when the shooting and screaming *did* begin on the steps of the building right under your window.

BUNTLOW

Well, we've never had any of that sort of thing at all. It's a very quiet neighborhood.

BARTLOW

Well, I'm sure your memory is playing tricks on you. We've heard several expert witnesses testify that at least five bullets were fired that night—and that the body of Gordon Bozlow fell right there on the steps in front of 2116 Willow Hollow Road. Surely you couldn't have slept through all that.

BUNTLOW

Well, I don't see why not. I live clear across town on Beach Street.

BARTLOW

Then what you're telling the court is that you're not the Pamela Buntlow who resides at 2116 Willow Hollow Road.

BUNTLOW

No—that's not who I am. But I believe there is another Pamela Buntlow here in town. She's a missing witness in a murder case or something like that. I'm not exactly sure.

BARTLOW

Very well. You may step down . . . and, Your Honor—the defense rests.

(*Theme establish and under for*)

RAY

So once again, justice prevails—thanks to the tireless efforts of the dedicated defense attorney. Join us again soon when the Inter-Mountain Baby Food Cartel—the world's largest packager of mooshed-up vegetables for your little one—will present more courtroom drama starring—Lupis Bartlow, Counselor-at-Law.

(*Theme up full and then out*)

BULLETIN

We recently announced that walnut pickers were urgently needed at the Follansbee Nut Ranch in Kernel County to harvest the walnut crop. We have been advised to notify prospective walnut pickers that while they may eat all the walnuts they wish . . . they MUST bring their own nutcrackers.

Our Song

BOB

With romance the keynote of the day, it's time for the "Our Song" department . . . interviews with sentimentalists who remember the song that lent impetus to their romance. And my card tells me that "our Songer" today is Mr. Leo Trasp of Picture Mount, Wyoming . . .

TRASP

Hello, Mr. Elliott.

BOB

Leo, nice to see you.

TRASP

I didn't think I was going to make it. Just before I came here I was stung by a wasp.

BOB

I see. Now, Leo, I think we'd all like to hear about your song . . . the one that means so much to you and your wife. Tell us the name of the song which made so much difference when you two were courting.

Bob sharing "Our Song" with a friend. Ray is dubious.

Courtesy of the Museum of Broadcasting

TRASP

Certainly. I remember the circumstances. Did you want to hear about them, too?

BOB

Yes, circumstances are important.

TRASP

All right. Well, the funny thing is ... I didn't even like Beulah when I first met her. It was in a shoeshine parlor, and she elbowed me out of the way so's she could get to the only available seat first.

BOB

I see.

TRASP

After that incident, Beulah and I started going steady. And she gave me a gift—a musical wallet which played "The Lamplighter's Serenade" when opened.

BOB

And that's your song, Leo?

TRASP

Certainly it is.

BOB

Well, it's a very tasteful song. And I imagine you and your wife spent a good many evenings opening your wallet and listening to "The Lamplighter's Serenade"?

TRASP

Well, it's the only wallet I own, and frankly, we're a little sick of the tune. We may send it to Switzerland for a refill. . . . We've got another song, too.

BOB

Just what is that, sir?

TRASP

Well, Beulah and I have always attached a great many memories to a song called "Comin' in on a Wing and a Prayer."

BOB

Oh, yes . . . the famous World War II song classic.

TRASP

Back then, we especially enjoyed the Harmon Pickett version of the tune, featuring Jim Pickett on the tenor sax.

BOB

I suppose you were an airman during World War II—with Beulah sweating out your safe arrival at some unknown and dirty airstrip?

TRASP

No. I wasn't in the service.

BOB

Then you and Beulah selected the tune purely on the basis of . . . what?

TRASP

Well, we picked it for . . . tune . . . originality of lyric . . . beat. . . .
It's not a bad tune, you know.

BOB

I agree. But I don't imagine you two get to hear it much these
days.

TRASP

Not as much as we'd like to. But, we have other favorites. No
sense sticking to one song if you can't hear it.

BOB

That's right. And what are some of those other favorites, Leo?

TRASP

"Tippy Tippy Tin"—there's a song that meant a lot to us. Ah . . .
"Perfidia" was another one we used to get sentimental about . . .

BOB

Now, where were you two when you first heard your song,
"Comin' in on a Wing and a Prayer"?

TRASP

Well, we were all over at my uncle's house, listening to the *War-
time Frolics* radio show.

BOB

Featuring Johnny Bench and the Four Half-Noters?

TRASP

That's right. And the Half-Noters sang "Comin' in on a Wing
and a Prayer," "Tippy Tippy Tin" and "Perfidia"—one right

after the other. And my uncle suggested that Beulah and I become sentimental about them.

                              BOB

Well thanks, Leo Trasp, for telling us about your songs . . . and
good luck, sir.

                    (*Quick playoff*)

Wall Street on Parade

(*Theme: "Pennies From Heaven." Establish and fade for*)

OFFENHOUSER

Welcome now to *Wall Street on Parade*—the show that reviews the complex world of finance in terms that small investors can understand. My name is Gordon Offenhouser. And here with me are the wizards of Wall Street we've all come to depend upon. We have Mr. Chalmers Boatwright, the senior partner of Boatwright and Boatwright. To his left is Mrs. Winona Fifer, the associate director of monetary things for the state of New Jersey. And down at the end of the table is our senior expert, Mr. J. P. Warmerdam. Mr. Warmerdam, of course, is the retired chairman of the Merchants United Eastern First Federal Manhattan Security Trust Company. And as we turn to the actions of the stock market during this past week—I think we might get an over-all appraisal from Mr. Boatwright.

BOATWRIGHT

Well, of course, we all know the market has been fluctuating recently, Gordon. And that's about what I expected. I think with short-term interest rates going as they are—we could figure that normal profit-taking would alternate with mounting concern over industrial production beyond fiscal 1985. I predicted that more than a month ago.

WARMERDAM

I don't understand.

FIFER

Well, I'd have to agree with our senior expert, Mr. Warmerdam. I don't understand either. A month ago, you weren't predicting anything of the sort, Chalmers.

OFFENHOUSER

Well, I don't know if that was the point Mr. Warmerdam was raising when he said he didn't understand, Winona. He was cupping his hand behind his ear as if to indicate that he didn't understand anything Chalmers was saying.

BOATWRIGHT

Yes. That was my interpretation, too, Gordon. I don't see it as a matter of verifying past performance. Of course, I'm not sure now where the Dow Jones average stood at the time I came out firmly. But it was obvious that a market correction was in order—unless we had a turnaround in the balance of payments situation to nullify it. And I was right on both counts there.

WARMERDAM

I don't understand.

FIFER

Well, I'm not surprised you don't understand, Mr. Warmerdam. I never heard such gobbledygook in my life. And all this happened the same week Chalmers was touting the railroad industry for a strong comeback. So I picked up a few hundred shares of Sheboygan, Oshkosh and Western—

OFFENHOUSER

Excuse me, Winona—but we try to refrain from mentioning specific stocks on the air.

FIFER

Well, I certainly wish Chalmers had refrained from opening his big fat mouth about that one. Sheboygan, Oshkosh and Western has gone from thirty-two down to four-and-a-half. I understand they don't even have enough cash to pay their brakemen this month.

WARMERDAM

I don't understand.

BOATWRIGHT

Well, I'm sure we can all appreciate why Mr. Warmerdam doesn't understand. It's common knowledge that the railroads have been phasing out their brakemen for several years. And if Winona is too dumb to realize that—she never should have bought stock in S. O. and W.

OFFENHOUSER

Well, I think we're getting a little off the point here, and—

FIFER

Well, I do, too. If it hadn't been the brakemen, it would have been somebody else. And Chalmers knows that. He should also be aware that the money I put up to follow his hot tip came out of my youngest boy's college education fund. That's Rupert—the one who's always dreamed of becoming a doctor.

WARMERDAM

I don't understand.

BOATWRIGHT

Well, I'm with Mr. Warmerdam on that one. I've met Rupert. And it's pretty obvious the kid's not playing with a full deck. So, as Mr. Warmerdam said, it's a mystery to all the rest of us why the boy should waste time in medical school.

OFFENHOUSER

Well, I don't know that Mr. Warmerdam made that statement directly, Chalmers.

FIFER

No. He certainly didn't. Mr. Warmerdam was just failing to understand why a smooth talker like Chalmers would tout a stock company that's about to go bankrupt. And that's especially unprofessional when he knows I'm a widow woman just scraping to get by.

WARMERDAM

I don't understand.

BOATWRIGHT

She means her husband is no longer living, Mr. Warmerdam.

OFFENHOUSER

Yes. I agree that's what Winona meant, Chalmers. And I'm sure we all join her in mourning her husband's passing. But now, our time is running very short. So in just a few seconds, Chalmers— could you summarize what you think we can look for on Wall Street in the week ahead?

BOATWRIGHT

Yes. I think we can look for the market to be closed on Friday. It's either Labor Day or Memorial Day. I always get those two mixed up.

OFFENHOUSER

Well, in either case, the result would be the same for the small investor. So I want to thank you and the other members of our panel for giving our audience the benefit of your keen insight. And I hope you'll all be with us again next time for another informative look at ... *Wall Street on Parade*. See you then.

(*Theme: "Pennies From Heaven"*)

Stretching Your Dollars

BOB

And speaking of small investors, not long ago we had as our guest the noted economist and comparison shopper, Mr. Holden Merkly. At that time, Mr. Merkly gave you listeners some valuable tips on stretching your dollars in these days of high prices. But we've received hundreds of letters containing more questions for Mr. Merkly. So he's kindly consented to come back today and answer some of those letters.

MERKLY

And I might add that it represented quite a sacrifice for me to do this. You know, I moved from New York to Idaho after I found that my utility bills would run at least thirty percent less out there.

BOB

Well, I hope the cost of a plane ticket to come back hasn't thrown your budget all out of balance again.

MERKLY

Oh, I never travel by plane anymore. I checked around to see where I could get the best buy for my transportation dollar. And I found that hitching a ride to New York from Idaho in the back of a poultry truck saved me well over a hundred dollars.

BOB

Well, that's certainly a bargain that I'm sure our listeners will want to remember.

MERKLY

I even caught enough loose feathers blowing around back there to stuff a pillow. So that represents another sizable saving.

BOB

Indeed it does. And I'm anxious to hear what other valuable tips you'll have to offer in answer to these questions from our listeners. ... This first inquiry on balancing the family budget comes from a lady who writes: "I've tried switching from meat to fish and then to chicken as my main dish. But now the price of everything is high."

MERKLY

Well, the housewife has to hunt for foods that are cheap because they're in season. And right now, those items would include fresh rhubarb, yellow squash and wild daffodils.

BOB

And you're recommending one of those things for a main dish?!

MERKLY

Well, not necessarily. You can also get those little gnarled, misshapen carrots quite inexpensively. Nobody wants them because they look icky and they're tough. But they can't kill you.

BOB

Well, I'm sure it would be an important factor in this woman's food shopping to find items that wouldn't kill her family. So I guess you've solved her problem—and we can move on to the next letter. ... This question comes from a man who writes: "I can't decide what to invest my money in, now that the rate of inflation is so high. Is there anything safe that will enable me to come out ahead?"

MERKLY

Well, sound investments with high yields are always hard to find. But I've made a thorough study of all the possibilities. And I feel that the safest things to invest in right now are a straight flush or four-of-a-kind.

BOB

Uh-huh. And I imagine the rate of return is good enough to keep you one step ahead of inflation, too.

MERKLY

Yes. Either of those investments should yield about four hundred percent profit in ten minutes—which is quite a bit more than most banks pay.

BOB

Okay. Well, that's another problem solved. And I think that leaves us just about enough time for one more listener's question. . . . This one comes from a lady who writes: "My children seem to outgrow their clothes almost as fast as I can afford to buy new ones. Have you ever found a solution to this problem?"

MERKLY

Yes— Indeed I have. There are a number of fine products on the market that will stunt a child's growth—and help cut down on clothing bills. Of course, it takes a bit of bargain-hunting because some of the exotic prescription drugs cost more than the shoes and blouses you want to avoid buying.

BOB

What about that stuff they use in the Amazon jungle to shrink skulls?

MERKLY

No. That just makes the child get smaller so his clothes don't fit again. It's obvious that you're no economist. . . . Personally, I've found that having each of my youngsters smoke eight or ten strong cigars a day works about as well as anything.

BOB

And I suppose that has the added advantage of keeping them too sick to eat nourishing food.

MERKLY

That's right. And then, too, you don't need expensive cigars. I did quite a bit of comparison-shopping on that—and I located a two-for-a-nickel panatela made in Taiwan that works just fine.

BOB

Okay. Well, I certainly want to thank you for dropping by and answering these questions.

MERKLY

Not at all. I was glad to be of help. And I'll just bill you for my services when I get home.

BOB

Fine—and you don't need to bother sending it air mail.

MERKLY

Oh, I never do that, I've found that it represents quite a saving when I just write on the envelope: "Postage will be paid by addressee." Good-bye.

(Footsteps and door closes)

Bank Announcement

BOB

As a public service, here's news for all you people who bank at the Friendly National Chemical Loan & Trust Company.

RAY

Several of the bank's branches have been moved, friends, and we'd be obliged if you'd make a notation of these changes.

BOB

First—the 79th Street branch of the bank has been moved to 147th Street.

RAY

The Wall Street branch is moving to Delancey Street, and will be known hereafter as the Canal Street branch.

BOB

The 32nd Street branch is now located at 95th Street.

RAY

And finally, the Fifth Avenue branch has been moved to Cicero Avenue in Chicago and hereafter will be known as the Outer Drive branch.

BOB

There's only one small problem that this all presents, and we feel it can easily be overcome with your help.

RAY

The folks at the Friendly National Chemical Loan & Trust Company have lost the records of the bank—the records of your deposits and withdrawals. Now, if you could come in to our main office at the corner of 57th and 11th and tell us *honestly* how much you have in there, we'd be much obliged. We'll take your word for it.

BOB

It sounds like a big problem, but it isn't really—if we all play fair and are honest about it. Thank you.

Dais Builder

RAY

Now, from TV convention center, here's Bob with a special live report . . .

(Carpentry sounds)

BOB

The opening of the big political convention draws ever closer, and activities increase daily among the many people behind the scenes who are busy preparing this great hall where the action will take place. One such gentleman is with me now . . . Mr. Grover Lundy—a builder of daises, music stands, lecterns and podiums. First, Mr. Lundy . . . would you tell us the function of each?

LUNDY

Well, we'll start with the dais. A dais is an elevation in the floor, or stage, built to accommodate one . . . or for that matter . . . twenty or thirty people . . . or even more.

BOB

An indeterminate number, you'd say?

LUNDY

Yes. I've seen as many as fourteen hundred people on a dais.

BOB

Where was that, Mr. Lundy?

LUNDY

Well, it was at a banquet in Torpid, West Virginia, feting the—

BOB

I know that town. But I didn't think there were that many people in it.

LUNDY

Actually, there aren't that many people in Torpid, West Virginia. There are only about seven hundred. But the local high school had a fourteen-hundred-piece band, and they were being feted that night.

BOB

And, I might raise an interesting point here, Mr. Lundy. Did the orchestra members have their musical instruments with them?

LUNDY

I was anticipating a question of that nature, Mr. Elliott. No, they didn't have their musical instruments with them.

BOB

Because, of course you understand—as I do—that if they had had their musical instruments with them, it would no longer be a dais, but in fact a bandstand. Isn't that correct, Mr. Lundy?

LUNDY

Yes. On the other hand, if a bandstand is unoccupied by musicians with instruments, it's called a dais.

BOB

Then, of course, a bandstand is built in tiers.

LUNDY

There are also tiered daises. I remember building a dais for a company banquet that had to accommodate about nine hundred officers of the firm. Now, if it had been built on one level, the employees would have had to crane their necks to see the officers. So I built a tiered dais.

BOB

You couldn't call that a bandstand, certainly.

LUNDY

Of course you couldn't.

BOB

Now, Mr. Lundy . . . what exactly is a podium?

LUNDY

Well, a podium is a square or rectangular block that's placed in front of an orchestra. And its function is fulfilled when it's stepped on by an orchestral conductor.

BOB

Prior to that time, it's just a block that's set in front of the orchestra?

LUNDY

Right. But, it's only used by symphony orchestra conductors. A cheap musician usually conducts from ground or stage level. It doesn't make any difference whether the band sees him or not.

BOB

I see. Now, a lectern?

LUNDY

Yes, that's where the speeches will be made. If the material placed on a lectern is to be read, it is referred to as a lectern. But if a musical score were placed on a lectern, you would then have to call it a kind of music stand.

BOB

Well . . . if a symphony conductor had his music on a music stand . . . but he wanted to begin proceedings by reading a few remarks to the audience, what would you call it then?

LUNDY

I guess you'd call it a musical lectern-stand.

BOB

That's what you'd call it, Mr. Lundy?

LUNDY

Once I've built a lectern, I don't care what they call it. If someone sees a dual function there, I would have to credit them with foresight and imagination.

BOB

By the way . . . just what would you call this spot in the convention hall that we're standing on?

LUNDY

I'd just call it the floor and let it go at that.

BOB

That, then, would be it for now from convention city . . . and back to the studio!

Presidential Hopeful

RAY

Yes, and speaking of politics, here's a guest from our studio audience; a gentleman who, they tell me, may well be the next president of the United States. My guest is Mr. G. L. Hummerbeck who—

HUMMERBECK

Excuse me. That's not Mr. G. L. Hummerbeck. It's The Right Honorable G. L. Hummerbeck!

RAY

Oh? You've already assumed the full title of the presidency, have you?

HUMMERBECK

No, not at all. It's just that my first name is The Right Honorable.

RAY

I don't quite get it . . .

HUMMERBECK

You see, I'm part Winnebago Indian. And they name a child after the first thing it sees when it's born. In my case, that happened to be the Right Honorable Charles Evans Hughes. He was Chief Justice of the Supreme Court at the time.

RAY

Well, that's a very interesting story, sir . . .

HUMMERBECK

Yes, it is. Of course, I've often thought it would be even more interesting if I knew why the Chief Justice of the Supreme Court was in our tent on the reservation the day I was born. But nobody seems to remember.

RAY

Well, in any case, it probably doesn't have much bearing on your current campaign to become president.

HUMMERBECK

No, probably not.

RAY

Which party's nomination are you hoping to win, sir?

HUMMERBECK

Well, I'm going after both of them. I think most politicians make a big mistake when they put all their eggs in one basket. And, I figure I double my chances by running on both sides.

RAY

I guess that's true—from a mathematical standpoint. But how can you run on a platform that fits either party?

HUMMERBECK

I stay away from the issues the others are talking about. Remember William Jennings Bryan? He ran on the free silver issue. Nobody seems to be doing much with that right now, so I've dug it up again.

RAY

I see. Well, I have no idea whether you can stir up any sentiment about free silver since the Hunt brothers tried to corner the market. I don't even remember what the issue was back in Bryan's time.

HUMMERBECK

Neither do I. But I read where Bryan got nominated after he made a big speech saying he wouldn't be nailed to a cross of gold. So I thought I'd say that, too, and see if it still works.

RAY

Well, of course, the statement may have had more meaning in those days.

HUMMERBECK

I doubt it. The important thing was that Bryan kept his promise. I looked it up in the library, and he never did let anybody nail him to a cross of gold. He just died of old age about twenty years later.

RAY

Well, I don't like to say this, Mr. Hummerbeck, but—

HUMMERBECK

You can just call me The Right Honorable. All my friends do.

RAY

Regardless—I'm afraid you come across as a man who doesn't know what he's talking about. And I imagine the voters of our state are smart enough to see right through you.

HUMMERBECK

Yes, I get the same impression. People here laugh at my speeches and heckle me a lot. But I plan to stick it out. See? My mother lives here, so I can stay at her place while I'm campaigning. And she doesn't charge me anything—even for doing my laundry.

RAY

So you'll come out ahead financially even if you're not elected president.

HUMMERBECK

That's right. To tell the truth, I didn't have the nerve to sponge off Mom and just hang around the house. But when the neighbors find out you're campaigning for president, they don't treat you like quite so much of a bum!

RAY

That's good devious thinking, sir. And now that you've explained your real reason for running, I know you'll pick up a lot of new support. Thank you, G. L. Hummerbeck . . .

HUMMERBECK

The *Right Honorable* G. L. Hummerbeck!

Consumer Affairs

RAY

We're inaugurating a new public service feature today. And a vital one it is, too, because our newest staff member is an expert in the field of consumer affairs. He's Mr. Hoyt Netley of Syracuse University. And I seem to have misplaced my sheet with your background on it, Mr. Netley. But I guess it's a safe bet that you're not the consumer affairs expert who's a former Miss America.

NETLEY

(*Chuckles*) No, no. I've been affiliated with Syracuse University for almost thirty years now. That's where I gained most of my broad experience in the field of product evaluation.

RAY

I see. And just what is it you do there at the university?

NETLEY

Oh, most anything that has to be done. Whatever needs attention around campus, somebody always says: —"Call Hoyt Netley. He'll take care of it."

RAY

Well, I guess a person could quickly become a consumer affairs expert that way.

NETLEY

Oh, yes. And in addition, I've been a consumer myself for many years.

RAY

Well, that's another feather in your cap then. And I see you've brought several products with you today to analyze for our listeners. I'm particularly interested in that thing there with the three wheels on it.

NETLEY

That's a child's tricycle that I'm recommending for its safety features. It's made in Denmark of polished hardwood. And you can see how the corners of each piece have been rounded off. That protects small children against a lot of the minor scratches they get from sharp points on metal tricycles—or even plastic ones.

RAY

Well, that's truly an important safety feature. And I hope I didn't sound foolish by failing to recognize the thing as a tricycle. But it doesn't have any pedals on it.

NETLEY

No. That's another feature. It doesn't have pedals.

RAY

Well, I guess that's for safety, too. But how does the child move it along without pedals?

NETLEY

It's really a whole new concept in tricycles. This little box under the seat is a simplified rocket engine that propels the trike.

RAY

You mean you put rocket fuel in this thing?!

NETLEY

No, no. Nothing that sophisticated. It works more like a simple Fourth of July skyrocket. A small charge of gunpowder goes in here. And the child just lights the fuse when he's ready to ride.

RAY

Well, don't you think it's kind of dangerous for a child three or four years old to be playing around with matches and gunpowder?

NETLEY

Oh, I don't know. I hadn't thought much about that aspect. I suppose a parent could supervise at first—and make the child aware of any possible danger.

RAY

Well, I suppose. But even so—

NETLEY

The instruction booklet says that the tricycle never attains a speed of more than fifteen miles per hour if the correct gunpowder charge is put in there. And, as I said before, the corners are rounded off in case the child should take a spill.

RAY

Well, I guess it's okay then. So what about these bottles you have lined up on the desk here? They seem to be different brands of headache remedy.

NETLEY

That's right. And they help me make a point that I don't think many consumers are aware of. Here on my left is a popular name-brand aspirin. One hundred five-grain tablets. And the price is around three dollars. Now, as you may know, this generic brand on my right is the same strength—with a price of only ninety-eight cents. But here's a third type I found today that you probably haven't heard of—Doctor Warblow's Tablets. The same five-grain strength—but one hundred for only twenty-nine cents.

RAY

Well, that seems like a good buy, Mr. Netley. But I notice the bottle has a skull and crossbones on it—and the label says, "For external use only."

NETLEY

Well, I think that's just one of those technicalities they got into with the Food and Drug people. You see, Doctor Warblow's Tablets are on the market as a preparation for making sheep dip. But they're the same five-grain strength as expensive pain relievers, so—

RAY

Well, I'm not sure they're exactly the same. The others all say they contain five grains of aspirin. But the label on Doctor Warblow's says that each tablet contains five grains of toxic sulfur.

NETLEY

Oh, really? I just saw the part about five grains. I didn't read the rest.

RAY

Well, I don't know much about chemistry. But I think "toxic" means it could be poison.

NETLEY

I'm not sure about that. All I can say is that two of them cured my headache this morning. And at twenty-nine cents, the price is hard to beat.

RAY

I agree. It's a real bargain for those who don't mind taking a chance.

NETLEY

Well, everything in life involves a certain amount of risk. I could walk out of this building and be hit by a bus. (*Chuckles*)

RAY

True. We can't isolate ourselves from every danger. So I want to thank you for the valuable tips you've shared with us today. And we'll all be looking forward to the next session with Mr. Hoyt Netley—our Bob and Ray consumer affairs advisor.

Einbinder Flypaper

RAY

Now ... an important message from the makers of Einbinder Flypaper. Friends—despite our rigid quality control system at the Einbinder factory, several thousand rolls of flypaper have been released to the public with stickum that could become defective under certain conditions.

BOB

If you've bought flypaper recently that bears the manufacturer's code number 3-8-2-9-3 ... or 3-8-2-9-4 ... return it to the plant for new stickum at once. And while you're waiting for it to be returned to you—better protect your family by going out and buying some new flypaper.

RAY

When you do, be sure you insist on genuine Einbinder ... the brand you've gradually grown to trust over the course of three generations.

BOB

By the way, there's still time to order Einbinder's beautiful lapel pin. It's a lifelike replica of a giant horsefly ... a pin that makes an ideal accessory for either ladies or gentlemen ... with all eight of its legs painted in gleaming black enamel.

RAY

The wings are a lovely transparent mother-of-pearl and there's a simulated emerald set right in the insect's hind quarters that's sure to gain compliments from all your friends.

BOB

You'll want to have one of these gorgeous pins for yourself and several more to give as gifts for almost any occasion. So stock up on Einbinder Flypaper now ... and send in your proof of purchase stickers.

RAY

But be sure you insist on genuine Einbinder ... the flypaper you've gradually grown to trust over the course of three generations!

BULLETIN

Earlier, we announced that walnut pickers were urgently needed at the Follansbee Nut Ranch in Kernel County. We wish to add that time-and-a-half overtime will be paid to those pickers who can pick walnuts with one hand, and keep smudge pots going with the other. In addition to attractive wages, transportation and free walnuts, nutpicks will be furnished to patriotic Americans who answer this call.

Garish Summit #1

(*Dramatic theme music. Establish and under for*)

BOB

Now, another chapter in the endless story of intrigue as it unfolds among the prominent families of Garish Summit. There—in stately splendor far removed from the squalid village below—they fight their petty battles over power and money.
(*Theme up briefly and then fade for*)

BOB

As our action begins, it is Christmas Eve at the Murchfield Estate—and the servants are holding their annual holiday party in the root cellar near the main house. Suddenly, the voice of Lloyd the gardener can be heard speaking out above the festive gaiety.

LLOYD

I sure hate these Christmas parties Miss Agatha makes us hold every year in the root cellar. It's way below zero in here.

WILFRED

Oh, I shouldn't be too critical of Miss Agatha, Lloyd. She's a good sort. Now, just pull up one of those bags of turnips and sit down. We're going to sing carols soon.

LLOYD

Keep your shirt on, Wilfred. I'm trying to find an ice pick to chip off a piece of eggnog. It sure would help if Miss Agatha put some electric lights down here.

WILFRED

Now, now, Lloyd. Miss Agatha's a good sort. Just try to get into the spirit of the holiday and—
(*Crash*)

LUCILLE

My word, Lloyd! You fell right in my lap.

WILFRED

Do stop flailing around in the dark and sit down on one of those turnip bags, Lloyd.

LLOYD

I still need an ice pick—but I give up. It really ticks me off that we have to celebrate Christmas down here. I can just picture the family up in the main house—all comfy.
(*Bridge with instrumental of "Good King Wenceslas"*)

RODNEY

Confound it all! I've rung three times for the butler to come freshen my brandy. Where is that slothful wretch?

AGATHA

Now, Rodney. Just sit down in your wing chair and relax. I told the servants they could have forty-five minutes for their Christmas party. So Wilfred's probably down in the cellar with the others.

RODNEY

It seems to me that you're terribly lax with the hired help during the holidays, Mother. I was especially upset when I got your memo today ordering me to close the lead mine an hour early just because it's Christmas Eve.

AGATHA

Well, I know it causes a drop in those production charts you keep. But your brother Caldwell said it was cheaper to close early than to risk another riot like the miners staged last Christmas.

RODNEY

I might have known that any scheme promoting idleness would have been Caldwell's idea.
(*Tinkle of bell*)

RODNEY

Confound! The servants still don't answer the bell. They're probably all drunk down there by now. I can just picture them.
(*Bridge with instrumental of "Jingle Bells"*)

LLOYD

Don't bother thawing out your eggnog over that lighted match, Wilfred. I just found it's been made with sour milk. Can you beat that! Miss Agatha made our Christmas eggnog with sour milk.

WILFRED

There, there, Lloyd. I'm sure it was unintentional. Miss Agatha's a good sort. Now, let's sing carols.

LLOYD

I've just about had it up to here with you, Wilfred.

WILFRED

Up to where? I can't see you in the dark.

LLOYD

Oh! Sorry! I'm pointing to my throat. I just don't understand why you always stick up for Miss Agatha when she makes us hold our party in this damp cellar. Even the turnips down here are rotten. Can't you smell them?

WILFRED

Yes. But I'm sure Miss Agatha didn't know—

LUCILLE

Are those rotten turnips? I thought it was Lloyd's after-shave I smelled.

WILFRED

This is no time for sarcasm, Lucille. I was just saying that Miss Agatha's a good sort—and fond of us all.

LLOYD

Ah, knock it off, Wilfred. Miss Agatha's an old bat. You're the only one who likes her—and I often wonder why.

WILFRED

Hopefully, you'll never learn why. I can just picture the problems it would cause if anyone ever found out.
      (*Bridge with instrumental of "Christmas Time in the City"*)

CALDWELL

Great Scot! I just found out why that slimy little butler is always fawning over Mother.

LAWYER PARDEW

Don't shout, Caldwell. The Airedale was sleeping by the fire, and you startled it. I don't see why you came here on Christmas Eve anyway, demanding to see your mother's legal papers.

CALDWELL

It was because I couldn't contain my curiosity about her early life, Mr. Pardew. And look what I found. A document dated 1943 that makes a British war orphan her legally adopted son. That son— now grown to manhood—is our family butler, Wilfred Llewelyn Nimby.

(Theme. Establish and under for)

BOB

Will Wilfred freeze in the root cellar before he can assert his rightful claim to a room in the main house? Can Mr. Pardew be bribed to destroy the only known copy of his adoption papers? And what about the Airedale that only pretends to be asleep? Perhaps we'll learn more next time we hear Lloyd the gardener say . . .

LLOYD

I didn't know you could make stuff out of fermented turnips that would pack this kind of a wallop!

BOB

That's next week when we resume our story of endless intrigue on *Garish Summit.*

(Theme up briefly and then out)

Mr. I-Know-Where-They-Are

RAY

Time now for another visit with Ralph Flinger . . . better known to us as "Mr. I-Know-Where-They-Are." The man who keeps track of the greats and near-greats who've dropped out of the limelight. Ralph?

FLINGER

Thank you, Ray, and good evening, nostalgia lovers.

RAY

Let's get right to some of those names from the past, Ralph. For instance, where is Harley Freeney, the famous Australian comedian?

FLINGER

Ah, yes, Harley Freeney. He was known as "The Will Rogers of Melbourne." He used to shear sheep and tell jokes at the same time.

RAY

Where is he today?

FLINGER

Well, he inhaled a good deal of wool over the years . . . and when he did his act in a theatre, he sprayed the audience with lint. But he's entering a sweater factory shortly to have the wool removed.

RAY

He's temporarily out of work, then?

FLINGER

Yes . . . but he'll never starve. He runs a unique smoke-shop service. He sells kangaroos with tobacco in their pouches. He settled in Australia to escape his creditors in Panama.

RAY

Okay. Here's another: do you know the whereabouts of Chester Cogwell, the developer of the sling chair?

FLINGER

He's still sitting in the first one he ever made, unable to get up.

RAY

Ralph, many years ago there was a marathon dancer named Bessie Farley . . . who danced for a solid year without stopping. What became of her?

FLINGER

She married a foot doctor from Chicago. Later she and her husband found they didn't care for Chicago, so they moved to Fort Lincoln, Nebraska . . . where they both are involved in visual education. They manufacture the pictures that go into those little telescopic eyepieces.

RAY

Do you know where Louis Gorby, the man responsible for the vent in the back of men's jackets, is today?

FLINGER

Interesting story. He got his idea by watching theatre curtains. It's somewhat the same principle. And when Gorby represented the idea as being his own, the theatre-curtain people sued and there was a legal battle that dragged on for years.

RAY

Who won?

FLINGER

The theatre-curtain people. The courts ruled that the vent was too much of a coincidence.

RAY

Where is Gorby today?

FLINGER

His exposure to the courts taught him a lesson . . . and he's now taking a law course at Clinker University in Canada.

RAY

Ralph, do you happen to know the whereabouts of Philip Tuckman, the once-famous engineer?

FLINGER

Tuckman. Wasn't he the chap who tried to prove that rolled-up paper had the tensile strength of steel?

RAY

That's the one. Where is he today?

FLINGER

Well, as you know, Tuckman tried to prove the theory by building a bridge made of paper.

RAY

And wasn't he the first man to walk across the bridge, Ralph?

FLINGER

Yes, on April 10th, 1939—forty-six years ago. And, as you know, he plummeted downward onto a barge ... with his bridge wrapped around him.

RAY

That's right. One newspaper account said he looked like a package as he dropped. Is he still with us, Ralph?

FLINGER

Well, the last I saw Tuckman, he was in Vancouver, British Columbia, working in the wheat fields. He was tan as a nut.

RAY

Gee, these are really fascinating memories, Ralph.

FLINGER

Aren't they, though?

RAY

How about Greta Swenson, the Channel swimmer?

FLINGER

She still swims, you know.

RAY

That's amazing . . . after all these years!

FLINGER

Yes. She's known as "the grand old lady of the crawl."

RAY

Where's Greta now, Ralph?

FLINGER

Well, she's swimming to Palm Beach, Florida, from New York City. She started in October of last year. It's taking her quite a while.

RAY

She must be over eighty, Ralph.

FLINGER

She is. And that's why we should overlook her slow time.

RAY

But do we know where she is at the present time?

FLINGER

Just before air time, a cutter reported spotting something gray in the water off Cape Hatteras . . . and it was moving slowly.

RAY

Well, let's leave it at that, then, Ralph. Greta is probably off Cape Hatteras. 'Fraid there's time for just one more. Can you locate Otto Von Romo . . . the famous old-time movie director?

FLINGER

He had a run of bad luck in 1928. The puttees around his legs became unraveled during a scene, and he tripped and fell on his megaphone . . . knocking out several teeth.

RAY

What happened to him?

FLINGER

A surgeon replaced his teeth with gold ones, and in a freak accident one night, an old prospector drove a claim stake into his mouth.

RAY

He was never the same after that?

FLINGER

Right. He went back to Germany and went into the machine gun business.

RAY

Well, thank you again, Ralph Flinger—Mr. I-Know-Where-They-Are—for helping us relive some great moments out of the past!

Ward Stuffer—Book Critic

BOB

It's time now for a report from Ward Stuffer, our roving literary critic. I believe today, Ward, we're going to discuss a book of military significance . . . but you look a little puzzled . . .

STUFFER

Well, during the past week, I've read fifty or sixty books that I couldn't put down until I'd finished them, a thing like that can keep you awake.

BOB

I understand. But, about the book you're prepared to discuss today?

STUFFER

Right. It's the war memoirs of a private, Bob, and it's entitled *Barracks and Brickbats*. It's by ex-PFC Franklin Hardy. I found it a very revealing book.

BOB

So did I. And, after reading it, I wondered how we managed to win World War II. Is the material about Sergeant Elmont Furze true, Ward?

STUFFER

Well, I checked out some of it, and the story about Staff Sergeant Furze *is* true, Bob.

BOB

Then it's a fact that Sergeant Furze was drinking malteds at the PX when he should have—

STUFFER

That's right. When he should have been supervising the scrubbing down of the barracks floor.

BOB

That's shocking, Ward.

STUFFER

Well, I talked to a lot of men who'd been stationed with Sergeant Furze at Fort Whalen in Georgia, and they all thought he was highly overrated as a military figure.

BOB

And about Sergeant Furze playing poker on April 12, 1943 . . . is that true, too?

STUFFER

Right. He was playing poker with some other military figures, about an hour before his men were due out on the parade ground for their calisthenics.

BOB

And that was one of the war's biggest military fiascos, was it, Ward?

STUFFER

Yes. Instead of playing poker, Sergeant Furze should have been telling his men where the parade ground was.

BOB

And because he neglected to do so, many of his men never reached the parade ground.

STUFFER

That's correct. And those men who did manage to locate the parade ground . . . well, they were totally unprepared. Many of them didn't even know what exercise was!

BOB

Ward, when you read the book, wasn't it surprising to you that a man like Furze was able to achieve the high military rank of staff sergeant?

STUFFER

Yes . . . Private Hardy discusses that in Chapter Six of his book.

BOB

Uh-huh.

STUFFER

Despite Sergeant Furze's shortcomings as a military leader, he was a first-rate opportunist and—

BOB

He was promoted to sergeant during his first week in the Army, wasn't he?

STUFFER

Yes. On his second day in the Army, Furze went over the hill. When he was brought back, he discovered his fellow soldiers had developed tremendous respect and admiration for him.

BOB

Leadership qualities?

STUFFER

Right. His commanding officer promoted him to sergeant the very next day.

BOB

Ward . . . after reading the book, do you feel the war might have been shortened if someone other than Sergeant Furze had been running things?

STUFFER

Well—I'm not here to . . . I mean, I'm a book reviewer, not a military man.

BOB

General Brookside read the book, and he said that if Sergeant Furze had been relieved of his command, the war might possibly have been shortened by fifteen or twenty minutes.

STUFFER

Well, as an Allied Commander, General Brookside made mistakes himself. I don't think any of us will ever forget the day he dropped three divisions of paratroops on London.

BOB

Well, only time and history will tell. But anyway, thanks for being with us, Ward Stuffer. We look forward to your next book review.

Search for Togetherness

(Organ soap opera theme in and under for)

RAY

And now, *Search for Togetherness* . . . the touching story of people just like yourself who struggle to find happiness in a small midwestern town . . . where the steel mill has been closed permanently.
(Organ surge then under again and out during)

RAY

As our action begins today, young Doctor Honeycutt is just unlocking his office upstairs over the cafe where Agatha is employed part-time. Suddenly, out of the shadows steps old Doctor Gilroy, the only other physician practicing in Roaring Falls.

GILROY

Well, I see you've finally arrived to unlock your office, Doctor Honeycutt.

HONEYCUTT

Yes. I have to do that before I can go inside because I keep it locked when I'm not here. What can I do for you, Doctor Gilroy?

GILROY

It's not a question of what you can do for me, Honeycutt. As I think you know, I'm a general practitioner of the old school. That means I give no quarter and I ask none.

HONEYCUTT

I wish you wouldn't make quite such a point of exerting your independence, Doctor Gilroy. After all, no man is an island.

GILROY

What's that supposed to mean?

HONEYCUTT

I really don't know. It's just one of those old sayings that seem to make the rounds here in Roaring Falls from time to time.

GILROY

Personally, Honeycutt, I make it a point never to pass along gossip like that—especially if I don't know what it means. I have a stern code of ethics when it comes to matters of that type.

HONEYCUTT

Has it ever occurred to you that perhaps you're just a little too rigid in your approach to life, Doctor Gilroy?

GILROY

Honeycutt—I didn't come here to discuss my own approach to life. I came to ask about your diagnosis in the case of the oldest Snyder girl. She's been to see you recently, I believe.

HONEYCUTT

Yes. But of course, I can't discuss a diagnosis without getting the patient's permission. I have a stern code of ethics when it comes to matters of that type.

GILROY

Has it ever occurred to you that perhaps you're just a little too rigid in your approach to life, Doctor Honeycutt?

HONEYCUTT

Nonsense! It's just that I learned a good deal from my father, who was a general practitioner of the old school. So, of course, he gave no quarter and he asked none.

GILROY

Well, that may have been acceptable in his day, Honeycutt. But remember, no man is an island.

HONEYCUTT

What is that supposed to mean?

GILROY

Well, in this case, it's a simple analogy. An island is a piece of land completely surrounded by water. So it must learn to survive on its own resources. But as human beings, we are much less self-sufficient. So that's where we get the saying: No man is an island.

HONEYCUTT

That's very interesting, Doctor Gilroy. I've heard that saying before. But until now, no one was ever kind enough to explain what it meant.

GILROY

Well, I remember your father, Honeycutt. And I'm sure he's the type of man who would have taken a moment to discuss it with you.

HONEYCUTT

No. I don't think so, Doctor Gilroy. He was a general practitioner of the old school. So, of course, he gave no quarter and he asked none.

GILROY

Well, I guess we all sensed that he was a little too rigid in his approach to life.

HONEYCUTT

Yes. He never learned that no man is an island.

GILROY

What is that supposed to mean?

HONEYCUTT

I'm not sure. It's just something I heard the oldest Snyder girl say when she was here in the office the other day. But then she fainted before I could ask her what she meant.

GILROY

I heard the oldest Snyder girl had fainting spells. That's why I stopped by to ask about your diagnosis of her case.

HONEYCUTT

I never discuss a diagnosis without getting the patient's permission. I have a stern code of ethics on matters of that type.

GILROY

Well, I'm sorry to hear that you've become so rigid in your approach to life, Honeycutt. Perhaps you'd do well to consider the fact that no man is an island.

(*Organ theme in with sting, then under for*)

RAY

And so old Doctor Gilroy has confronted young Doctor Honeycutt directly. But will Doctor Honeycutt choose to confront the charge of inflexibility that Doctor Gilroy has confronted him with? Perhaps we'll learn more in the next episode. Join us then for more exciting drama on . . . *Search for Togetherness.*

(*Organ theme up to big finish*)

Down the Byways ...
With Farley Girard

(*Theme: "Merrily We Roll Along." Establish and then fade for*)

RAY

Now, through the magic of live radio, we present *Down the Byways*—a nostalgic journey into some corner of America with Farley Girard. Today, Farley has parked his deluxe motor home in Fairfield, Illinois, to bring us his homespun report. So come in, Farley Girard.

GIRARD

For those of us old enough to remember, there will always be a dim recollection of wonderful visits to the corner candy store. A handful of pennies could buy a lot of dreams down there. And we made our selections carefully as we inhaled the sweet, musty smell of licorice whips and horehound balls and lemon drops.

DANKS

(*Background*) Will you get to the point?! I'm trying to run a business here.

GIRARD

Just a moment. I need to create the mood first.

DANKS

(*Background*) Well, step on it. Wires strung all over the place here.

GIRARD

For most of us, those expeditions for jawbreakers and ju-jubees are now made only in memory. But for the children of Fairfield, Illinois, a little bit of vanishing America is still alive—thanks to the efforts of one man—a man named Merle Danks.

DANKS

Just to speed this along, let me say that all I set out to do was keep a little bit of vanishing America alive here. You know—someplace where kids could buy goodies for a penny like I did when I was a boy. I always tell people that's what motivated me to keep a little bit of vanishing America alive right here in Fairfield.

GIRARD

Well, truly the ingredients of another time are all around us in this smalltown emporium of wonders. And, Mr. Danks, I suppose these earthenware crocks are jammed full with licorice sticks and lemon balls and those other marvels of an earlier day.

DANKS

No. Actually, licorice sticks and lemon balls run into quite a bit more money nowadays than the average child can afford. So I sell those by mail in my Christmas gift packs. They start at $6.95 and run all the way up to $23.50.

GIRARD

That much, eh?

DANKS

Well, I've got a big overhead to cover. Those four-color holiday catalogs don't come cheap. And every year, there gets to be more competition from other places selling all kinds of nostalgia stuff.

GIRARD

Uh-huh. Well—

DANKS

There must be a thousand of them in Vermont alone.

GIRARD

Probably. But it's the wonderful things you store in these earthenware crocks to sell to local children for a penny that interest me. . . . You do keep something in these for the local children, don't you?

DANKS

Oh, you bet I do. A big variety of items—mostly produce from the local grocery that's just a little too overripe to sell to the general public. Like this stuff here.
(*Clatter of crockery lid being lifted*)

GIRARD

Gee, that's kind of disgusting, Mr. Danks. Are those decaying oranges in there?

DANKS

Either oranges or tangerines. It's hard to tell when they get to this point.

GIRARD

Well, whatever they are, I can't believe that children would want to buy them.

DANKS

Well, they're not real keen about buying them. But I just tell them that for a penny they can't be too choosy. Of course, I also stock bananas that have turned kinda black—and grapes that have gone mushy—whatever's in season.

GIRARD

But all basically garbage.

DANKS

Yeah. I guess you could call it garbage—although that word has kind of a negative connotation. And you gotta remember—it's hard to make money selling anything that's even halfway edible for a penny.

GIRARD

Well, you don't seem to be selling anything anyway. You haven't had a customer since I've been here.

DANKS

That's true. But you should have been here yesterday. I got in a shipment of stale, broken ginger snaps. And I sold the extra-soggy ones for a penny apiece. When the neighborhood kids heard about that, two or three of them flocked in.

GIRARD

Clutching their treasured coins in their little fists, were they?

DANKS

Oh, yeah. It would have warmed your heart to see them. Grubby faces—and with their little noses running.

GIRARD

And so the eyes of Merle Danks light up as he thinks of the youngsters who patronize his little store tucked away here in a corner of the Midwest. Merle Danks is one of those who thinks of profit not in dollars—but in the smiles of children. His is a vanishing breed. And we're glad we found him as we traveled on—*Down the Byways*. And now—as we head out to see what may lie over the next rise in the road—this is Farley Girard saying so long for now.

(*Play off with "Merrily We Roll Along"*)

Amnesia

RAY

We have a gentleman here whom we've agreed to interview in the hope that one of you viewers may recognize him. As I understand it, sir, you are suffering from complete amnesia?

MAN

Well, I'm not really suffering like you say you're suffering when you hurt someplace. Actually, I'd say I feel better than average if I could remember how I used to feel when I felt average.

RAY

But you can't remember anything . . . which indicates you're suffering from amnesia.

MAN

Well, I'm not really. You say you're suffering when you hurt someplace. In fact—

RAY

Yes, sir. You told us all about that.

MAN

Did I? That's funny. I don't remember it. I must be suffering from amnesia.

RAY

Yes, you are. Maybe we should give the public a complete physical description of you. In your own words, how would you describe yourself?

MAN

Well, in my own words, I'd say I'm about twenty-eight or thirty years old, above average height—quite trim, but very muscular. I have a sort of Robert Redford-type profile . . . and to the best of my knowledge, I'm unmarried.

RAY

Well, to the best of my knowledge, you're in your fifties, you stand five foot seven, weigh 175 . . . and bear a striking resemblance to a cocker spaniel.

MAN

Oh. But you do agree that I'm probably unmarried.

RAY

That could be. Now. Do you have any recollections at all of your past? Any shred of evidence that might help to identify you?

MAN

Well, as evidence goes it's not a really good-sized shred—but I do keep getting one mental picture.

RAY

Any little thing might help.

MAN

You see, I get this picture of me as a child all dressed up in velvet knee pants and like that. And I was playing around with some toys on the floor of a great big room.

RAY

That might indicate you were raised in a large house then.

MAN

I'd say it indicates more like it was a palace. Then, I remember a soldier rushing in and saying to Mumsy: "Marie Antoinette, your Royal Highness, the revolutionaries have almost got the place surrounded. You'd better smuggle the kid out of here to America while there's still time!" That's about all I remember.

RAY

Well, of course, if that's what you really remember, it would mean you're Louis the Seventeenth—the rightful King of France who disappeared during the Revolution.

MAN

I was hoping you'd think that's what it meant. So if you'll just sign this affidavit, I'll catch the next plane to Paris and take over.

RAY

I think I'd be more likely to sign a warrant for your arrest instead. You see, Louis the Seventeenth disappeared from France two hundred years ago.

MAN

Gee, no kidding? I guess I forgot to notice the date when I looked it up. Maybe I'd better check on somebody more recent—but just as rich—that I could be!

RAY

Maybe. In the meantime, I want to apologize to all you viewers for taking up so much of your valuable time with this impostor. . . . Back to you, Bob!

Music Contest

BOB

We've been checking out our competition up and down the radio dial this week to see what we might do to add a few more listeners to our vast audience. And I think we've come up with just the thing.

RAY

That's right. We found that a lot of other radio shows give prizes to listeners who can identify a mystery tune that's played on the air. And we thought a contest like that might be good for us, too.

BOB

Of course, this comes as wonderful news to those of you at home because Ray and I have each chipped in five dollars to be awarded to our first mystery tune winner.

RAY

But that's just the beginning, friends. Our chief studio usher, Herbie, has generously donated his 1958 Studebaker as a major prize. And today's contest winner can claim it simply by having it shipped from the repair garage in Springfield, Ohio, where it's now scattered around the floor.

BOB

All told, it's a contest jackpot worth almost one hundred dollars. So listen carefully, and see if you can be the first to call our special Bob and Ray Mystery Tune phone number with the correct title of this song:
(*Music: The first four or five notes of "Begin the Beguine"*)

RAY

Okay. That's it. And now, we're standing by our special phone to see if we have a lucky winner. (*Very brief pause*) I guess not. Maybe next time.
(*Phone rings*)

BOB

Just a minute, Ray. We seem to have a contestant. . . . Hello.

OPERATOR

I have a person-to-person call for the Bob and Ray Mystery Tune phone number. Is he there, please?

BOB

Well, that's not any one particular person. But I can take the call.

OPERATOR

Your party doesn't seem to be there, sir. Will you speak with anyone else?

MAN

Yeah. Anybody is okay. The name of the song is "Begin the—"

OPERATOR

Just a moment, sir. You'll have to deposit one dollar and thirty cents for the first three minutes.

MAN

Oh . . . okay.
> (*Methodical plink of coins dropping into the phone.*
> *Continue through the following.*)

RAY

What's going on?

BOB

He seems to be calling from a pay phone.
> (*Plink of coins stops*)

OPERATOR

That was only a dollar twenty, sir. You need to deposit another ten cents.

MAN

Gee. I don't have any more change. Could I mail it to you?

OPERATOR

Certainly not. Don't talk nonsense.

BOB

Operator, we're on the air here. Can't we just accept the charge and get on with this?

OPERATOR

You keep quiet. This doesn't concern you at all.

MAN

Just a minute. I found another dime. Here you are.
> (*One more plink of coin dropping into phone*)

OPERATOR

Thank you. Go ahead, sir.

BOB

Hello . . . hello . . . Operator, we've been disconnected.

OPERATOR

No, you haven't. I can hear him fine.

BOB

Well, what's he saying?

OPERATOR

He's saying he's been disconnected. Apparently, you're not talking loud enough for him to hear you.

BOB

I don't think that's the problem. I can't hear him either.

OPERATOR

Well, for pity's sake. I don't know what the two of you are doing.

MAN

Hello . . . hello.

OPERATOR

My word! You people—

BOB

Just a minute, operator. I can hear him now. Hello, sir. Can you hear me okay?

OPERATOR

Yes. He says he can hear you just fine.

BOB

Well, now I can't hear him again. Just ask him to name our mystery tune, and then tell me what he says.

OPERATOR

Oh, very well. But there should be an extra charge for this service. . . . He wants you to name some tune or other for him. . . . All right. Hang on. . . . Hello, New York.

BOB

Yes.

OPERATOR

He says it's been so long since he heard it that he forgets how it goes. Could you hum it for him?

BOB

No. And he wouldn't be able to hear me, even if I did. So just cancel the call.

OPERATOR

You can't cancel the call, buster. He paid for it.

BOB

Well, that's between the two of you to work out. But we'll be carrying our treasure chest of prizes over until next time, when we'll add a big five dollars to it, and try again for a winner in our Bob and Ray Mystery Tune Contest.

BULLETIN

This is the last call for walnut pickers at the Follansbee Nut Ranch, Kernel County. The walnut harvest will be in full swing in a matter of hours, and in cooperation with the American Walnut Commission, we urge you to contact the ranch at once. Wire cable address: "Nuts," Kernel County, at once, and receive free transportation and recipe for walnut pudding.

Vanishing Animals

(Theme: Exotic, African-type music. Establish and under for)

BOB

Welcome again to *Berne Voyle's Vanishing World of Vanishing Animals*—today combing the plains of the African veldt in search of the elusive warthog.
(Theme up briefly and then fade for)

VOYLE

(Deep and profound) Among the repulsive animals of the world, the warthog has always held a particular fascination for sportsmen and other people alike. And so it was that our group set off by motor launch up the Zambezi River in quest of this curious specimen of nature.
(Squawking birds and general jungle sounds under)

VOYLE

Slowly, we plied our way through the dense rain forest that the natives have long referred to in their native tongue. Across the former colony of Mozambique we struggled upstream, one slow mile after another. Then, suddenly, my chief launch driver appeared on the poop deck—full of excitement—to utter the words the whole crew had been waiting to hear.

DRIVER

Simba! Simba, bwana!

VOYLE

What he was saying was true. We were indeed coming to that bend in the river that separates Mozambique from Zambia. But, in a larger sense, it also separates the rain forests of the down-country from the open grassland of the upcountry. In short, we were nearing the home of the warthog.
(*Hog snorting and oinking*)

VOYLE

Our caravan's assistant box lifter, Bernie, was the first to sight one of the elusive animals. And he rushed to me—full of excitement—with the news.

BERNIE

Warthog, bwana! Warthog!

VOYLE

The warthog has roamed the plains of the African veldt for perhaps twenty million years. Not the same individual warthog for that whole period of time—to be sure. But ugly beasts quite similar to the ones we know today were there—rolling in the mud long before man.
(*Hog snorting and oinking*)

BERNIE

Warthog, bwana! Warthog!

VOYLE

(*Shouts*) All right already, Bernie! I saw him! (*Returns to deep monotone*) To learn more about this interesting animal, we sought out the director of Rhodesia's Bumbomwee Field Station, Nigel

Wainscoat. Nigel has spent more than half his colorful life study-
ing the ways of the vanishing warthog here in the veldt—far away
from civilization. And he spoke very eagerly about his favorite
subject.

WAINSCOAT

(*British*) Well, I should say the ruddy warthog is thriving here in
Bumbomwee. You can see the specimens over there in the corral.
They're each being marked to trace their migratory patterns.

VOYLE

Mr. Wainscoat pointed off toward the field station's warthog corral. And we saw for the first time the animal-marking program he
had just told us about. The male warthogs were being injected
with green vegetable oil on their muzzles—and the females with
purple. Our host happily explained the field station's reason for
carrying out such a program.

WAINSCOAT

Many outsiders think it's a bit senseless to inject green vegetable
oil into the muzzles of the male warthog—and purple into the
muzzles of the females. But we've given the matter a good deal of
thought. And we have our reasons for doing it.

VOYLE

During a later conversation with Mr. Wainscoat, we explained
the long-range project our camera crew had undertaken: to photograph all of the world's vanishing animals, birds and reptiles in
their natural state while a few still remained. He expressed both
surprise and amusement to hear of our undertaking.

WAINSCOAT

(*Chuckles*) Oh, I say! That is a good one. Making this long journey
to photograph the warthog in the belief that it's a vanishing spe-

cies. (*Chuckles*) Oh, my! I'm sure the chaps in the pest-control division will get a chuckle out of that one.

VOYLE

Mr. Wainscoat went on to explain that the warthog population in the Bumbomwee district has grown from eight hundred thousand at the time of the Ibo Revolution to almost sixteen million today. The figures were in sharp contrast with what we'd been led to believe before we left home. And so we hopped back into the motor launch to begin our long journey back up the Zambezi. Mr. Wainscoat saw us off at the boat landing with a final word of farewell.

WAINSCOAT

Good-bye.
> (*Squawking birds and general jungle sounds under*)

VOYLE

Two days out of Bumbomwee, our crew was back into the rain forest. For the better part of a week, we pushed on—one slow mile after another. Then, suddenly, my chief launch driver appeared in the wheelhouse. He was full of excitement as he uttered the words we had all been waiting to hear.

DRIVER

Simba! Simba, bwana!

VOYLE

What he was saying was true. We were indeed cruising through the fashionable suburbs of Dar es Salaam. And soon we'd be back at the motel enjoying such luxuries as a hot shower with running water. Our long journey in quest of the vanishing warthog was over, at last.
> (*Theme. Establish and under*)

BOB

This has been *Berne Voyle's Vanishing World of Vanishing Animals.* Join us again soon when Berne and his loyal crew will take us up the frozen walls of Mount Everest in search of the bushy-haired goat—another vanishing animal from this vanishing world of ours.

(*Theme up briefly and then out*)

The Hobby Hut

(*Theme: Bouncy type. Establish and fade during*)

BOB

Now let's pay another visit to the Hobby Hut, the special feature conducted by Neil Clummer, editor of *Wasting Time Magazine*. Neil is nationally known as Mr. Hobby himself. I see his guest has arrived, so let's join them . . .

CLUMMER

Thanks, Bob . . . and greetings, hobbyists everywhere. My guest today is Mr. Mulford B. Thaxter, of Skokie, Illinois—who's one of the leaders in his field: collecting numbers from places where they ask you to take a number. Right, Mr. Thaxter?

THAXTER

Well, Neil, I'm a little too modest to call myself a leader in the field. But I do have over twelve hundred numbers from places where they ask you to take a number . . . and that's about three times the size of the next largest collection.

CLUMMER

Well, then, I'd certainly say that makes you a leader in your field. And I'm sure our audience would like to know how it all got started.

THAXTER

Like so many great things, it was an accident. One hot summer day about four years ago, I took my little boy, Mulford, Jr., to an ice cream parlor near our house. When I saw a thing on the counter that said: "Please take a number to be served," I naturally took one.

CLUMMER

And that was the beginning of your collection, eh?

THAXTER

Not right away, Neil. See—I hadn't planned to keep the number. It was this big plastic one—the kind they use over and over. I just wanted to hear the number called—then I would gladly have given it back.

CLUMMER

Well, something must have happened there to turn you from an ordinary consumer into an avid hobbyist. What was it?

THAXTER

The number I took was 72. And the next one the clerk called was 56. As I say, it was a hot afternoon and the place was crowded—

CLUMMER

And your little boy was whimpering for ice cream—

THAXTER

Yes, that was the real key to the thing. I knew Mulford, Jr., couldn't wait until they'd served everybody from 56 to 72. So I started to put my plastic number back on the rack and leave . . .

CLUMMER

And something stopped you?

THAXTER

Some other people had come in and taken numbers. So that made 75 the next card showing on the rack.

CLUMMER

... Presenting the problem of whether to put your number back or just take it with you. So you took it, thus starting your collection.

THAXTER

Right. How did you know? Have I told you this story before?

CLUMMER

No ... I just guessed that might be the ending. But it's still hard to imagine how you'd get twelve hundred examples for your collection ... in just four years!

THAXTER

Well, when you just take a number and leave—it doesn't take nearly as long as taking a number and waiting to be served.

CLUMMER

That figures.

THAXTER

Also, I get specimens from other collections all over the world. Like this. It's from a hobbyist in Russia, and the prize of my collection.

CLUMMER

I can see why. The Russians seem to make their number tickets out of woven straw. The number on this one is 2541—which certainly would indicate that consumers have to wait longer to be served than we do here.

THAXTER

Yes. The gentleman who sent me this ticket said it came from an auto showroom. I guess they have quite a shortage of new cars there. He wrote that he'd have to wait about four years to be served if he ever took a number to keep for himself!

CLUMMER

You know, it's really interesting when numbers have stories like that to go with them.

THAXTER

I'll say. Here's the oldest one I have, dating back to the time of the Oklahoma Land Rush. It's carved out of wood . . . and the number on it is "one."

CLUMMER

One?

THAXTER

It was used, I'm told, in a remote area where the storekeeper only had two customers. So he only needed one ticket—in case he was serving a customer . . . and the other one came in.

CLUMMER

That's ridiculous, Mr. Thaxter.

THAXTER

I know. I made up that story. You said they were interesting!!

CLUMMER

I'm sure the viewers appreciate your effort to make the collection seem more interesting than it is . . . and thanks for being with us in the Hobby Hut! Have a good day—and find a good hobby! Everyone?

(Fade in theme—up and out)

The Bob and Ray Overstocked Warehouse

RAY

And we have a terrific announcement to make now! Bob and Ray have another blockbuster for you.

BOB

We've told you before about our big warehouse that's always bursting with war surplus bargains?

RAY

Well, last night it really burst . . . and what a mess. But our loss is your gain. We have exactly 164 bayonets, complete with scabbards, which were never used during the war!

BOB

That's right. They were sent back from Cuba right after the battle of San Juan Hill . . . absolutely untouched.

RAY

But that's not all. We have 322 pairs of canvas leggings which were used only once . . . at the battle of San Juan Hill.

BOB

What's more: these leggings were used only going *up* the hill, not down.

RAY

We have 214 pairs of heavy-duty campaign boots, sizes twelve, fourteen and seventeen. And some of these match. All of them have only slight mud stains from San Juan Hill.

BOB

And that's not all. We have thirty-six flagpoles which fit the hand perfectly. If you plan to run up a hill on your vacation, waving a flag, don't miss this bargain!

RAY

And listen to this, fans. We have exactly twenty-two slightly used ammunition wagons . . . which were damaged just a bit when they slid back down San Juan Hill. A few nails here and there . . . some bicycle tape . . . a coat of paint . . . a little grease . . . and you can take your own ammunition with you when you go on vacation.

BOB

Finally, we have 124 full cases of canned corned beef, which are clearly stamped San Juan Hill, 1898, on the tops of the cans. If you do not find this corned beef all you had hoped it would be, just leave word with the executor of your estate to return the remaining unopened cans to us.

RAY

If you want to snap up some of these terrific war surplus bargains . . . write today . . . to Teddy Roosevelt, care of New York, New York!

Fern Ock Veek

(*Organ theme. Establish and fade for*)

BOB

And now the Burnside Corporation, celebrating its golden jubilee year in bankruptcy, brings you another episode in the adventures of *Fern Ock Veek, Sickly Whale Oil Processor*—the heartwarming story of a typical Eskimo coed from U.C.L.A. who seeks a new and more meaningless life in the wilds of Alaska. As our scene opens today, Fern has just been released on bail while she awaits her trial for auto theft. She is busily carving a pagan idol out of a walrus tusk in her isolated cabin when Officer Wishmiller of the Alaska State Highway Patrol enters.
(*Door opens. Wind howling. Door slams*)

FERN

Oh, it's you, Officer Wishmiller of the Alaska State Highway Patrol. How nice to see a familiar face. I was just busily carving a pagan idol out of a walrus tusk in my isolated cabin here.

WISHMILLER

Well, I'm glad you found some way to take your mind off your problems, Fern. I'm sorry I can only stay a minute, but I just wanted to stop in and give your a piece of advice.

FERN

Well, you can just leave it there on the table and I'll look at it as soon as I finish my carving. If I don't get this pagan idol in shape to face it toward Anchorage by sundown, it won't do a bit of good.

WISHMILLER

Fern, I can't leave the advice I want to give you on the table. I didn't write it down.

FERN

Well, I guess I can knock off for a minute to hear you out—even though I'm not legally obligated to let you waste my time until after our forthcoming marriage.

WISHMILLER

I understand that, Fern—but this is for your own good. I hear the D.A.'s got an open and shut case against you on that auto theft charge, and I think you'd better forfeit your bail and leave the state while there's still time.

FERN

Well, that doesn't sound like a very practical idea to me, Officer Wishmiller. My bail was five hundred dollars, and that pile of junk I stole wasn't worth more than seventy-five clams at the outside. I think I'd be coming out loser all the way around if I just blew my investment and blew.

WISHMILLER

Fern, you've let yourself get so wrapped up in the economics of this thing that you forget a conviction could put you in stir for five years.

FERN

Well, I admit that's a point worthy of some consideration. I suppose I could go back to U.C.L.A. and hide out for a while. So many of the students there are on the lam that they'd never notice one more.

WISHMILLER

That's a great idea. And even if they did find you, you'd be in another state and could fight extradition.

FERN

No. If I recall, I fought him once and he knocked me cold in the third round. I certainly don't want any more of that.

WISHMILLER

Fern, I think you have extradition confused in your mind with Muhammad Ali. But we don't have time to straighten you out. Just toss a few things in a suitcase and you can still catch the 5:30 businessman's economy flight to Los Angeles.

FERN

Well, I guess maybe that would be the best thing to do—even though I'm too much of a muddy thinker to know for sure. I just assume you'll join me there at your earliest convenience.

WISHMILLER

Well, that's hard to say, Fern. I'm not sure the Alaska State Highway Patrol has a branch in Los Angeles. But if it does, you can bet your boots I'll pull every string I can to put through a transfer.

FERN

And no matter how long it takes, I'll be waiting.
                    (*Theme. Establish and under for*)

BOB

Will Fern's plan to catch the 5:30 businessman's economy flight succeed even though she's not a businessman? Can Officer Wishmiller tolerate the loneliness of being the only Alaska State Highway Patrolman on duty in California? And why hasn't the mysterious owner of the car Fern stole noticed that it's missing yet? Join us next time when we'll hear Fern say:

FERN

I don't have any idea what I'm doing here. I didn't even know that Alaska Airlines had a flight to Leningrad.

BOB

That's in the next exciting episode of *Fern Ock Veek, Sickly Whale Oil Processor.*

(*Theme up briefly and then out*)

Speaking of Names

RAY

We've been rummaging through the old phone book again to come up with an interesting subject for our *Speaking of Names* feature, and we've found one. Welcome, Mr. Marco—

POLO

Polo. It's pronounced the same way.

RAY

Our guest, indeed, is Mr. Marco Polo, of 3416 Pendleton Place, Brooklyn, New York. Were you surprised when we notified you by mail?

POLO

About what?

RAY

About being invited to appear on our show.

POLO

Oh, no, I wasn't surprised. But it's lucky I was invited here on a Thursday. I couldn't have made it at any other time.

RAY

Well, that's when we do our broadcasts here . . . Thursdays.

POLO

Then it was lucky for both of us.

RAY

Mr. Polo, if you've listened to our show, you know we ask our guests what happens to them because of the famous names they have. Now . . . are you any relation to the Marco Polo of yester-year?

POLO

No. Although a good many people seem to think I'm related to him, and they make demands on my valuable time.

RAY

What do you do for a living, Mr. Polo?

POLO

I'm a bobsled designer.

RAY

And I suppose that keeps you busy a good deal of the time?

POLO

Not as much as you'd think.

RAY

Now, Mr. Polo . . . you mentioned before that demands are made on your valuable time. Quite frequently, I believe you said. Do people call you on the telephone?

POLO

Yes, they do. Yesterday I got a call from the Fontaine Boot and Toe Club.

RAY

The famous walking society?

POLO

That's right. The society marched from Schrafft's 96th Street up to the water fountain located at the southeast corner of Van Cortlandt Park and they asked me to meet them there and give a talk.

RAY

And all because your name is Marco Polo.

POLO

That's right.

RAY

I guess you told them you weren't related to the real Marco Polo at all?

POLO

That's correct, too. But they didn't seem to mind. They wanted me to meet them at the water fountain anyway.

RAY

Well, I read somewhere that this is National Walk Week, and there's a drive on for new members. What other demands are made on your time because of your name, Mr. Polo?

POLO

Well, we aren't quite through with the Fontaine Boot and Toe Society . . .

RAY

Oh. What else did they want, Mr. Polo?

POLO

They intend to put out a semiannual pamphlet called the *Marco Polo Digest*.

RAY

And what sort of material is there to be in the pamphlet?

POLO

Oh, offbeat walking routes . . . maps of interest . . . nature trails, and special mud reports. Plus some other stuff not quite as interesting.

RAY

And I suppose they want permission to use your name?

POLO

That's right. And for the use of my name, they're offering me a free membership in the Society . . . plus a lapel button made up in the likeness of Vasco da Gama holding a compass and a shoe.

RAY

And are you going to give them permission to use your name?

POLO

I don't think so.

RAY

It must be a nuisance, being bothered by phone calls all the time, Mr. Polo.

POLO

Yes. And even though I'm listed in the Yellow Pages, too, I rarely get a caller who wants a bobsled.

RAY

That's not at all unusual, Mr. Polo. I know of a golf course builder who was listed in the Yellow Pages. He didn't get a single call in five years.

POLO

Yes—but when he does get an order, it must keep him busy for at least ten years.

RAY

I suppose so, Mr. Marco Polo. And I'd like to thank you for being with us today on ... *Speaking of Names.* Can I give you a lift? I'm going north—

POLO

Which way is that?

RAY

Forget it!

BULLETIN

A final correction: In that call for walnut pickers to harvest the walnut crop at the Follansbee Ranch in Kernel County, the crop has just matured, and it turned out to be cashews. We wish to apologize for this error, and urge you to continue to listen to our future announcements, made in cooperation with the American Cashew Commission.

Chatting With Chesny

RAY

Welcome now to the new Bob and Ray public service feature, *Chatting with Doctor Chesny*. We're inviting all of you disturbed listeners to call in and receive expert advice on your personal problems from the noted psychologist Doctor Merton Chesny. And before we begin, Doctor, I just want to say that we all feel honored to have you here with us.

CHESNY

Really? Perhaps you'd care to probe deeper and find out why you feel that way.

RAY

Well, I think it's pretty obvious. You're a leader in the field of experimental psychology. And you've headed that department at a large Eastern university for ten or fifteen years now.

CHESNY

It's fourteen, actually. During that time, I've placed almost sixty thousand guinea pigs in cages of various colors. That was done to determine the effect of environment on their behavior.

RAY

Sounds fascinating. What did the experiment prove?

CHESNY

Well, of course, I had to allow for a laboratory error of up to three percent in my findings. But even so, there is solid evidence that the color of the environment has no bearing on behavior.

RAY

I see. And I suppose that would hold true for human beings, too.

CHESNY

No. That only applies to guinea pigs. I think they may fail to react because they're all color-blind. But I haven't checked that out.

RAY

Well, in any event, it's a scientific breakthrough. Now, I see that our phone is lighting up with the first call from a listener who's seeking your advice with a problem. So why don't you carry on, sir?

CHESNY

Fine. I'd certainly prefer that to what we've been doing. So I'll pick up Line One here. . . . Hello. You're on the air with Doctor Chesny.

MAN

Hello. My name is Luther C. Pocter and I—

CHESNY

Please, sir! Don't tell me your name.

MAN

Oh . . . okay. I'm an anonymous party. And my problem is my two sons, Hubert and Skipper. They're real jealous of each other.

CHESNY

A sibling rivalry, eh?

MAN

No. It's more like when we have pig's knuckles for dinner, and one of them gets the last knuckle. Then the other one always throws a tantrum and claims I'm playing favorites. I just hate that.

CHESNY

Well, it's up to you as a parent figure to be evenhanded. For example, if one of your boys gets a bit more food, you can show the other that you love him just as much by giving him a bath toy or some small trinket.

MAN

I guess that might work. But I'm not too sure.

CHESNY

Well, the only alternative is administering firm discipline.

MAN

Oh, I could never get away with that. You see, Hubert's thirty-seven now and Skipper's thirty-four. So they just threaten to punch my lights out if I try to boss them around.

CHESNY

I see. Well, I'm sure the insight you've gained from our little talk today will help you work out something. Now, I must move on to another call from a person in need. . . . Hello. You're on the air with Doctor Chesny.

WOMAN

Oh, I'm so glad I got through to you, Doctor. It's about Leonard.

CHESNY

He's your husband, is he?

WOMAN

Oh, my, no. I mean Leonard Nimoy. Every night I dream he shows up at my house with one of those unexplained phenomena he talks about on TV. Sometimes he brings the abominable snowman. And last night it was a whole family of creatures with fish scales from the Bermuda Triangle.

CHESNY

And naturally you wake up terribly frightened.

WOMAN

More upset than frightened, really. I'd like to have a little time alone with Leonard. But he always brings these weirdos with him. I don't even know what to serve them to drink.

CHESNY

Well, of course, I can't waste my time advising you how to be a good hostess. So I'll move on to another caller who's more in need of my help. . . . Hello. You're on the air with Doctor Chesny.

MAN

Hello. I'm a gentleman with a wild look in his eye who hasn't come out of his room in twenty-seven years. Is that anything to be concerned about?

CHESNY

I suppose it might be a symptom of something deeper. How do you feel about the situation?

MAN

Well, I don't have much time to think about it. I got married recently, and we're expecting our first child. Also, my career in computer software is moving right along. And I've gotten my golf handicap down to three strokes.

CHESNY

I thought you said you hadn't been out of your room in twenty-seven years.

MAN

It's a very large room.

CHESNY

Well, if you're happy there—

MAN

I'm not entirely happy. I'd like a dog. But when I order one by mail, they send the runt of the litter. And, of course, I'm afraid to go to the kennel and pick one out in person.

CHESNY

Well, many people are afraid of dogs—and with good reason in the case of the larger breeds. So I'd say that your reaction is quite normal. And I hope I can offer that same reassurance to others in our next session. Until then, this is Doctor Merton Chesny wishing you all good luck and good emotional stability.

Feature Story Follow-ups

RAY

As you may know, one of the public services we occasionally perform is satisfying your curiosity about those little one- and two-paragraph feature stories that appear in newspapers.

BOB

The papers run those human interest items every day. But they never seem to follow up on them later to let us know how the stories came out. So, periodically, we track down some of the people whose stories have appeared—and bring them here to New York so they can tell you what eventually happened. Our first guest was the subject of a United Press feature story several months ago. And you're Mr. Hubert Wedlow of Harrisburg, Illinois. Right, sir?

WEDLOW

Yes. That's correct. I became involved in one of these humorous foul-ups that computers are always making. And of course, the newspapers love to print feature items about that subject. I understand I got almost two full inches of space in more than four hundred papers coast-to-coast.

BOB

Well, that's more publicity than most of us achieve in a lifetime, Mr. Wedlow. And I understand that the computer mistake in your case was made on your weekly paycheck.

WEDLOW

Yes. I work for the gas company back home. And I'm supposed to make one hundred and sixty-two dollars a week. But then, one week the machine went haywire and issued me a check for ten million, one hundred and sixty-two dollars. Of course, I knew right away that it was a mistake—I couldn't keep the money. But I showed the check to a local newspaper before I gave it back. And the editor made quite a fascinating item out of it.

BOB

Well, I'm sure many of our listeners saw that original item. But then we never heard how your story came out. Were you rewarded or promoted for your honesty in giving back that ten-million-dollar check?

WEDLOW

No. I was fired the next week. You see, the boss's wife is in charge of the payroll department. And the boss thought I should have come to him quietly—instead of pointing out coast-to-coast how his missus was a dimwit for not catching a mistake like that.

BOB

Well, it's obvious from your shabby appearance that you haven't been able to find another job. But we thank you for coming clear to New York to tell us the sad conclusion of your story. . . . For our next feature story follow-up, we have with us Mrs. Clara Shumbaw of Moberly, Missouri. And I understand the Associated Press ran a picture as well as a feature story about you, Mrs. Shumbaw.

SHUMBAW

Yes. They had a photographer right on the scene at the Missouri State Fair when I won a blue ribbon for my giant cucumber. It was almost two feet long and it weighed more than nineteen and a half pounds.

BOB

Well, I remember seeing the picture in the paper. And the cucumber really was enormous. But I'm wondering what happened after that original story appeared. Did you sign any contracts to display your giant cucumber at other fairs?

SHUMBAW

No. In fact, the newspapers had barely hit the streets when we cut the thing open and found out it wasn't a cucumber. It was a watermelon with bumps on the outside. I can't imagine how it got mixed in with my cucumber display—and I felt awfully silly about the whole thing.

BOB

Yes. I can see how you would. But you were a good sport to come here and tell us all about it. . . . Now, with today's last feature story follow-up, here is Mr. Herbert Botchford of Cleveland, Ohio. And, Mr. Botchford, I understand that the item about you appeared in almost nine hundred newspapers.

BOTCHFORD

Yes. It was in the *Cleveland Plain Dealer* originally. But then it was picked up by one of the national news services. And I heard later that it was also carried throughout the British Commonwealth by Reuters.

BOB

Well, that's amazing coverage. And just what was your story that attracted so much attention?

BOTCHFORD

Well, I went out to my mailbox one day last April. And I thought it was kind of funny that one of the letters had real old Christmas seals on it. But then, I also noticed that there was just a two-cent stamp on the front. So I examined the postmark very carefully.

BOB

Yes. I know you did. And to make a long story short—

BOTCHFORD

Well, I don't usually make it short when I'm telling it.

BOB

No. I'm sure you don't. But we're running out of time. So what it all boils down to is that you received a letter that had taken fifty-seven years to be delivered—even though it was mailed right in the same city.

BOTCHFORD

Yeah. That's right. It was mailed in 1928. The post office people can't figure out what happened to it all those years. But it finally turned up and got delivered.

BOB

Well, it's a mystery that may never be solved. But one thing you could clear up for us, sir. The news story didn't mention who the long-lost letter was from.

BOTCHFORD

It was from the Internal Revenue Service—telling me I owed another ten bucks on my 1927 income tax.

BOB

Well, I'm sure that small debt was canceled after you explained what happened.

BOTCHFORD

No. You see, figuring compound interest for all those years—I now owe $9433.67. And I can't pay it. So I'll be starting my prison term next week.

BOB

Well, then I'm glad we caught up with you while you're still available. And I want to thank you and our other guests for stopping by today so we could learn how your feature stories came out.

The Financial Advisor

BOB

Every week, we receive thousands of letters from you listeners, begging for our advice on how to invest your life savings.

RAY

Oddly enough, Bob and I don't feel qualified to give recommendations of that kind—in spite of the obvious success we've had in piling up several hundred dollars for ourselves over the years. So we've brought in an expert to answer your questions about investment.

BOB

That's right. He's Doctor Rex Latchford of Columbia University. And I presume, sir, that your doctorate is in economics.

LATCHFORD

No. I'm a veterinarian. So, of course, that allows me to use the title "Doctor" even though I don't have a private practice.

BOB

I see. You gave up your practice to teach at Columbia, did you?

LATCHFORD

No. I'm not affiliated directly with Columbia University. I just mentioned to you on the phone that my office is there—maybe six or seven blocks off campus—maybe a mile at most.

BOB

Uh-huh. So then you do have an office even though you don't practice veterinary medicine there.

LATCHFORD

That's right. My principal business is distributing those little foam rubber trinkets that you can hang from the rearview mirror of your car. But I'm also a notary public. And, of course, that's what led me into the field of investment counseling.

BOB

Well, that's certainly understandable. I've heard that many of the experts we see on *Wall Street Week* also started out as notary publics. . . . Now, I see that the first call from a listener is coming in on our private financial line. So why don't you take over, Doctor.

LATCHFORD

Fine. I'm always anxious to help those who have extra money lying around. . . . Hello. You're on the air with Rex Latchford.

MAN

Hello. My name is Eddie, and I'm a self-employed subway conductor who—

LATCHFORD

Excuse me, sir. Before we get to your question, I forgot to say earlier that I put out a weekly advisory sheet called the *Latchford Letter*. That's where I reveal my surefire strategy for tripling your money in less than a year. A four-week trial subscription to the *Latchford Letter* is available for only twelve dollars.

MAN

That sounds pretty good. Will the trial subscription give me all the tips I need to triple my money?

LATCHFORD

No. As I said, the trial subscription period is only four weeks. The part about tripling your money comes farther into the year. Our annual subscription rate is one hundred and forty dollars.

Courtesy of the Arizona Bank and Benton & Bowles, Los Angeles

MAN

Oh . . . Well, in that case, maybe I'd better ask my question now. You see, I answered an ad that said I could make big bucks addressing envelopes at home. And so far, I've addressed about fifteen of them. So I need to know how to invest my profit when it starts rolling in.

LATCHFORD

By any chance, did you pay a fee to those people who advertised that you could make big bucks addressing envelopes at home?

MAN

Only thirty dollars. I signed a promissory note for the seventy-five I still owe them.

LATCHFORD

I see. Well, now that I've learned more about you, I think you might be a good candidate for my investment program in tungsten futures.

MAN

Oh, no! No way! That sounds like a con game for real suckers. Isn't tungsten that cheap stuff they put in light bulbs to make them come on when you flick the switch?

LATCHFORD

If that's your question, you need an electrical engineer—not a financial analyst. So just get off the line and go check the Yellow Pages. . . . Now I see we have another call coming in. Hello. You're on the air with Rex Latchford.

CHILD

Hi. My name is Dickie Ritzman, and I've saved up almost fourteen dollars from mowing lawns and raking leaves.

LATCHFORD

Fine. Just send it to me in care of your local station, and I'm sure they'll forward it.

CHILD

Well, okay—if you think that's best. And thanks a lot for your time and trouble.

LATCHFORD

That's all right, son. I get a lot of satisfaction from working with young people. Now, we have time for just one more quick call. . . . Hello. You're on the air with Rex Latchford.

MAN

Hello. I'm calling long distance from Hibbing, Minnesota.

LATCHFORD

Well, I hope you dialed direct. That's a money-saving tip of mine.

MAN

Thanks a lot. But I'm thinking in terms of bigger dough right now. You see, I think I recognize your voice. And I can pick up a fast thousand-dollar reward if your name used to be Shifty Wayman before you changed it to Rex Latchford.

LATCHFORD

I'm afraid you're taking up the counseling time of someone who needs my help more urgently, so—

MAN

Excuse me. I misinformed you. My wife says the reward is two thousand now. The widows you cheated have gotten together and added to the original thousand put up by our local merchants.

LATCHFORD

Well, I'm afraid you have the wrong number—and we're running
out of time for this week, so—

MAN

It wasn't just your voice that gave you away. I was pretty sure I
had the right crook when you mentioned tungsten futures. That
was the same scam you used here in Hibbing.

LATCHFORD

So, until next we meet, this is Rex Latchford—your Bob and Ray
financial analyst—wishing you a good day and good investing.

Happy Birthday, Ken Vose

BOB

Thank you, Rex, and the best of luck wherever you end up. Now it's time for one of our most popular features. We like to chat with the more interesting members of our studio audience whenever we can, and we picked this gentleman—Ken Vose—because we learned it's his birthday. Welcome, Ken.

VOSE

(*Jovial—good-fellow type*) That's right, Bob. It is.

BOB

Happy birthday!

VOSE

Thanks.

BOB

What's your line of work, Ken?

VOSE

I'm kind of a trouble-shooter, Bob. I work as a liaison between management and employees. I see to it that the combined efforts of each side produce the maximum result.

BOB

Sounds important. Do you have a formula for doing this?

VOSE

I think so. I feel that a successful business is like a happy family, Bob. No one member can make it work. It's pulling together . . . sharing the load . . . teamwork.

BOB

Sounds like you know what you're talking about, all right. By the way . . . what do you want for your birthday?

VOSE

I think this may surprise you, Bob.

BOB

Oh?

VOSE

Believe it or not . . . I wouldn't care if I didn't get a single gift for my birthday. What do you think of that?

BOB

I'm taken aback. Why is that, sir?

VOSE

I'll tell you why. I don't need any gifts. I've already got the best gift a man could ask for. A lovely wife, four lovely children. What more could I possibly want?

BOB

You aren't interested in material things, eh?

VOSE

No, sir.

BOB

Well, that's certainly refreshing, but . . .

VOSE

No, I mean it! (*Pause—laughing*) Gosh! I just thought how stuffy I must sound. I mean . . . sure, I'd accept a gift. That's common sense. But, on the other hand . . . what better gift is there than to come home to a lovely wife and four lovely children after the toils of the day are behind you?

BOB

Well, I've got to admit—

VOSE

No question about it! Beats any gift I know. And it all adds up to one thing. Teamwork. Pulling together.

BOB

You know, Ken, I feel clean just talking to you. Let me shake your hand!

VOSE

Sure. Gosh! I ought to call Sally and the kids and tell them what a nice guy I met here.

BOB

Thanks. Er . . . where are they, Ken?

VOSE

They're out in Tacoma, Washington. That's where our home is.

BOB

Gee, I know how you must miss them. Are you here on a business trip?

VOSE

No. My company has more or less placed me here on a permanent basis. Been here for . . . let's see . . . eleven years now. I have an apartment here in New York.

BOB

Well—how often do you get to see the wife and kids, Ken?

VOSE

Not as much as I'd like to, Bob. It's quite cold out there.

BOB

Do they come to New York to see you often?

VOSE

Well, they may have. I'm not in my apartment all the time, and it's possible they could've missed me. But I never got any messages . . . so I don't think they came here.

BOB

Well, thank you for talking with us. I think we can all learn a lesson from you.

VOSE

Sure thing!

Planning Your Vacation

RAY

If a walking tour across Death Valley is included in your vacation plans this year, please heed these words of advice from the Department of the Interior:

BOB

The water supply in Death Valley is limited. In fact, for hundreds of square miles it is nonexistent. Therefore make sure you have a FULL canteen of water—with a leak-proof cap—before starting your walk.

RAY

As a matter of fact, the Department of the Interior would prefer that you don't walk across Death Valley at all, since footprints can mar the natural beauty of this pristine desert.

BOB

A word to the wise is sufficient.

RAY

That it is, Bob. And, it will soon be summer vacation time again for many of us. We're already starting to receive letters from listeners asking our advice on where to go and what to do. So we've invited well-known travel expert Mr. Godfrey Blandish to stop by and help us launch the brand new Bob and Ray public service feature—*Planning Your Vacation.* Mr. Blandish, I know you've spent most of your career in Britain. Do the people over there have as much trouble deciding where to spend their vacations as Americans seem to?

BLANDISH

(*British*) No. Not in the least. You outlanders here in the colonies take a much more provincial view of travel than those of us in the mother country. Of course, our long heritage of ruling the Empire enables us to see most things in a broader sense.

RAY

Well, what you're saying then is that you don't get silly questions from British vacationers because they know more about geography.

BLANDISH

No. I'm saying that we don't get silly questions from British vacationers because the crumbling of the Empire has left us all too poverty-stricken to travel anywhere.

RAY

Well, I can see how our provincialism could lead to a level of prosperity that you people don't have to cope with. And on that note, we might move along to the first question from one of our provincial listeners. . . . To begin this session of *Planning Your Vacation,* I have a letter here from a woman in Kansas.

BLANDISH

A letter from Kansas! I wonder if I might bother you for the stamp. I'm still missing most of the Pony Express series.

RAY

Well, this envelope doesn't have a pony express stamp on it.

BLANDISH

That's most peculiar. I wonder how it got here from Kansas.

RAY

I really don't know. As you said, we Americans are all very provincial. And I've never even thought about how mail gets to New York from the rest of the country. But anyway, this woman writes: "I'm planning a trip to Europe this summer, and can't decide whether to go by steamship or by air. I can get a direct flight from Wichita to London. But, of course, no ocean liners dock in Kansas. Do you think it's worth the bother of changing in New York just to go by ship?

BLANDISH

Well, I think it's simply appalling that your frontier still has no direct steamship connection with the mother country. The people out there must be in frightful need of supplies right now.

RAY

Well, I think they may have found some other way to get supplies in. It's just that they still can't get ocean liners out. But you seem to be recommending that this woman make the trip by air anyway.

BLANDISH

Oh, indeed yes. Especially if she's a female traveling alone. I don't believe I've ever seen a program on the telly where Indians attacked a caravan of airplanes.

RAY

No. I never have either. So let's go on to the next question. . . . This letter is from a man in Delaware who writes: "I've heard that the changing of the guard at Buckingham Palace is quite spectacular. Do you advise switching my European travel plans around just so I can be there when it happens?"

BLANDISH

Well, I should like to make one point quite clear. This man is not the first American hoodlum who's thought he could sneak into the palace while the guard was being changed. But I can assure the rowdy that he'll see the inside of Scotland Yard a good deal sooner than he'll make it inside the gates of Buckingham Palace.

RAY

Well, Mr. Blandish, there's no indication that this letter is from a hoodlum who wants to sneak inside the palace. He'd just like to watch the changing of the guard.

BLANDISH

The same way your Bonnie and Clyde liked to watch the changing of patrolmen in the vicinity of a bank, I dare say.

RAY

Well, I don't really think—

BLANDISH

Our constables are not the bumblers that Perry Mason has proved your American police to be. And finding oneself in Old Bailey is no jolly tea break either. We have ways of dealing with the creature who wrote this letter and others of his ilk.

RAY

I see. Well, I think the rest of our mail is all from creatures of the same general ilk. So I'd might as well skip it, and just thank you for your time.

BLANDISH

Not at all. I consider it a patriotic duty to keep as many undesirable aliens out of Britain as possible. Cheerio.
(*Footsteps and door slam*)

BULLETIN

RAY

We have been asked by the management to make the following announcement:

BOB

If anyone has seen a canoe drifting on the lake with red and white trim, and the name "Petunia" on it, please notify Mr. Harrison B. Oglivie at Wildwood cottage, 346 Ring 2.

Garish Summit #2

(Dramatic theme music. Establish and under for)

BOB

Time now for another visit to Garish Summit, and its endless story of intrigue among the socially prominent. There—in stately splendor far removed from the squalid village below—they fight their petty battles over power and money.
(Theme up briefly and then fade for)

BOB

As our action begins, the hollyhocks at the rear of the Murchfield Estate are being carefully pruned by Lloyd the gardener. Suddenly, a young boy enters the grounds over the barbed wire fence nearby. Lloyd puts down his pruning shears and speaks.

LLOYD

Hey! You'd better climb right back over that fence, young fellah. Miss Agatha turns the dogs loose on trespassers around here.

SPANKY

Oh, she wouldn't do that to her own flesh and blood. You see, I'm Spanky Murchfield, the grandson she doesn't know she had because my father is her son, Caldwell, who doesn't know I exist. It all happened by a previous marriage.

LLOYD

I didn't know Miss Agatha had been married more than once.

SPANKY

She hasn't. I'm talking about Caldwell's previous marriage. Incidentally, I assume you are Lloyd the gardener.

LLOYD

That's right. But how did you know my name?

SPANKY

Oh, I've done some research on all the hired help. You see, I plan to inherit the Murchfield billions by replacing Miss Agatha's authentic will with this forgery. But I need a trusted person on the inside to make the switch. How about it?

LLOYD

Oh, I couldn't. I've been mowing and edging for the Murchfields since 1938. I'm like one of the family. And when I retire, Miss Agatha's going to charge me very little rent to live in that old shed behind the barn.

SPANKY

Don't bore me with sentiment, pal. I'm proposing a big deal here. I've saved up almost twenty-six dollars. And it's all yours—just for putting this phony will in the safe.

LLOYD

Well, that does sound like easy money. And come to think of it, I never did like Miss Agatha's two sons, Rodney and Caldwell. I wonder what that boorish lout Caldwell would be doing right now if he knew about your scheme to cut him out of the old lady's will.

(*Music: bridge*)

WILFRED

(*British*) I can't believe what you're saying, Master Caldwell. I've been Miss Agatha's trusted butler for over thirty-two years. And now you're suggesting that I break the servants' code of honor.

CALDWELL

Ah, don't be such a Boy Scout, Wilfred. I just got a tip that Lloyd the gardener plans to substitute a fake will for Mother's real one. So all I want you to do is replace the forgery with this one—naming me as sole heir.

WILFRED

No. It just wouldn't be cricket for one who has made a career of domestic service. Besides—if I may say so, sir—you've struck me as something of a creep ever since you came here claiming to be Miss Agatha's long-lost son.

CALDWELL

You'd better watch your mouth, or you could talk yourself out of some big money. I borrowed fifty thousand bucks from petty cash at the office today. And it's all yours if you can slip this bogus will into the safe.

WILFRED

I say! That is a most generous offer, sir. And of course it would serve the purpose of cutting off your arrogant brother, Rodney, without a cent. I wonder what that wretched blighter would be doing right now if he had any notion of your clever scheme.
(*Music: bridge*)

THUG

Cheez, I dunno, Rodney. Will your brother really get all the dough if I can't slip this fake will into the old lady's safe?

RODNEY

Yes, Fingers. I'm certain that he's bribed Wilfred the butler to re-place the forgery that my nephew Spanky has bribed Lloyd the gardener to put in the safe, replacing the original. So, of course, the next step that must be taken is obvious.

THUG

Maybe. I'd have to think about it, and I'm not too long on brains.

RODNEY

Never mind. Money is what does the talking in cases like these. How much do you want to open Mother's safe in the library to-night and substitute this fake will for the other one?

THUG

Well, let me figure. I'd have to buy new wire clippers to get through the fence. . . . Then figure three bucks' worth of meat to keep the guard dogs quiet . . . a skeleton key for the front door. . . . All told, I guess nine million, eight hundred thousand dollars would do it.

RODNEY

I was hoping for an estimate that would run a little lower.

THUG

Well, look at it this way. If the job's done right, you'll get a fifty-room mansion, the family business and about three billion in cash. But if the job's done wrong, you'll get ten years in the slam-mer. So just ask yourself: is it worth pinching pennies?

RODNEY

No. I suppose not. Of course, it may take most of the afternoon for me to embezzle nine million, eight hundred thousand dollars from the firm. But somehow, cutting my evil brother off from the family fortune makes it all worthwhile.

(Theme. Establish and under for)

RAY

Will Rodney regret hiring a sleazy crook who doesn't have references from a previous employer? Can Lloyd the gardener succeed in cracking a safe with no tools except his pruning shears? And how can Spanky explain his absence from school? Perhaps we'll learn more next time when we hear the family attorney say . . .

PARDEW

Her real will was the one I kept at my office. It leaves everything to her pussycat.

RAY

That's next week when we resume our story of petty bickering on *Garish Summit.*

(Theme up briefly and then out)

Speaking Out

BOB

Now, it's with great pride that we again present the almost-award-winning Bob and Ray public service feature—*Speaking Out*. This is the portion of the show where we give you, the listener, a chance to phone in with your opinion on some controversial issue of the day.

RAY

That's right, friends. We're showing incredible generosity by donating our broadcast facilities and valuable air time, just so you can tell the world how you feel about current affairs.

BOB

You no longer need to shoulder your burden of concern about national events all alone because we're here to help shoulder it with you.

RAY

Well, that's kind of an overstatement, Bob. We let most of the grim topics that these people discuss go in one ear and out the other. But it gives them the satisfaction of knowing that they've probably ruined the day for a lot of other listeners.

BOB

Yes. That's the main public service we perform. And it could happen only in America. ... Now, I can see from the flashing light on the phone that we have our first caller. Would you give us your name please?

MAN

Yes. My name is Vidal Sassoon. And I live in Dearborn, Michigan.

BOB

Really? I thought you probably lived in California.

MAN

Well, I used to. But then the authorities had me extradited to Michigan.

BOB

I see. Well, then you're obviously not the same Vidal Sassoon.

MAN

That's exactly what I told them when they found me with the matches and gasoline can. But they sent me back to Michigan anyway.

BOB

Well, in any event, it probably has nothing to do with the opinion you called in to give us.

MAN

Probably not. The opinion I called in to give is that Calvin Coolidge won the presidential election of 1924.

BOB

Well, I'm not sure that's an opinion, sir. I consider it a fact.

MAN

Well, I did, too, until recently. Then I made some phone calls at random, asking people who they thought won the presidential election of 1924. And only nineteen percent said Calvin Coolidge.

BOB

I see.

MAN

Franklin Roosevelt and General MacArthur both scored higher than that. Also, there were some scattered votes for Rudolph Valentino—Fibber McGee—the Andrews Sisters—and Red Grange.

BOB

So your poll leads you to believe that the 1924 election is still un-
decided. Is that it?

MAN

Well, I'd say it's certainly too close to call. And we may not know
until we hear from the traditionally conservative western states.

BOB

Well, maybe you can report back then. And right now, we'll chat
with another caller. Your name please?

WOMAN

I'm Mrs. Wanda Guber of Roanoke, Virginia. And it's my opinion that my husband is stepping out with another woman every
time he claims he's going bowling.

BOB

Well, that's not really a controversial issue of major importance,
ma'am.

WOMAN

Not now, maybe. But it's going to become a controversial issue of
major importance when I catch him. You can rest assured of that.

BOB

Okay. Well, we'll try to reopen the subject when you can give us
more details. But for now, let's try one final quick call from another listener. Your name, please?

MAN

I'm Shaky Dopflyer. And I live in a furnished room at Mount
Rushmore—right under Thomas Jefferson's left ear.

BOB

Okay. And what's the opinion you want to give us, sir?

MAN

Well, I don't think Babe Ruth ever hit sixty home runs in one season. I'm convinced that it was all done by an impostor who didn't want his true identity known.

BOB

Well, do you have a theory on who that person really was?

MAN

No. Everybody's accounted for that I've been able to check out. I just know it wasn't really Babe Ruth.

BOB

Well, do you mind telling us what makes you so sure?

MAN

Not at all. The real Babe Ruth was a lady golfer. She never played professional baseball at all.

BOB

Are you sure you aren't thinking of Babe Zaharias?

MAN

Oh, yeah. I guess maybe I am. And here I've spent most of my adult life checking out my theory. Now I'll have to start all over again.

BOB

Well, I believe I have good news for you, sir. You won't have to start all over again because you've proven to the satisfaction of everyone listening that your whole premise is wrong. So I'm glad we could be of help. And I hope the rest of you listeners will feel free to share your opinions with us on the next edition of *Speaking Out.*

Phone Call to Anywhere

BOB

Just before show time, we picked a member of the studio audience to take part in our little game called *Phone Call to Anywhere,* and try for some of the prizes we have. The winner is Mr. Matt Neffer . . .

NEFFER

Thanks, Bob.

BOB

Now, you know the object of our little game, sir. You have to keep the party at the other end of the phone on the line for at least three minutes.

NEFFER

I understand.

BOB

And I believe you picked Cleveland, Ohio, for your try at a Phone Call to Anywhere?

NEFFER

Yes, I did. To my friend Al Twombley.

BOB

Okay, Mr. Neffer. The operator has your party on the line now, and remember . . . you must keep him there for at least three minutes! Here's the phone . . .

NEFFER

Hello, Al? This is Matt.

AL

Hiya, Matt. . . . Where are you?

NEFFER

I'm in New York City. I'm calling from New York City. Are you home, now, Al?

AL

I picked up the phone, didn't I? I must be home.

NEFFER

Well . . . look around and make sure.

AL

I don't have to look around. I'm home. I can see my wife and kids.

NEFFER

Well, I'm here in New York City, Al.

AL

Well, I'm here in Cleveland. In my home.

NEFFER

Where?

AL

Where what?

NEFFER

Where in your home are you?

AL

Oh, I'm in the living room, Matt.

NEFFER

I see. (*Long pause*) Al . . . the last time I talked to you in Cleveland . . . you told me you were going to move. Did you?

AL

No. I'm still living in the same place here. My old home in Cleveland.

NEFFER

I see. (*Pause*) Al . . . did I ever show you my wristwatch?

AL

Lots of times.

NEFFER

Well . . . you should see it now.

AL

I can't, Matt. I'm in Cleveland.

NEFFER

That's too bad, Al. Because the watch looks altogether different now. It's on Eastern Daylight Time.

AL

Well, I'll take a look at it when you get back to Cleveland.

NEFFER

All right. (*Pause, then aside*) Is three minutes up yet? (*Shakes head*) No, huh? Er . . . Al?

AL

Yeah?

NEFFER

If I forget to show you the watch next time I get to Cleveland, you'll remind me, won't you, Al?

AL

Well, if I remember, I will.

NEFFER

Look, Al . . . tell you what.

AL

What?

NEFFER

I may forget to show you the watch . . . and you may forget to remind me . . . so . . . ah . . . suppose I mail you the watch . . . and then, when I visit you, I can pick it up and show it to you.

AL

Well, if I got your watch in the mail, you wouldn't have to show it to me. I could open the package and I could take a look at it then . . . right on the spot.

NEFFER

I see. (*Pause*) Well, then. . . . This is what we'll do: I'd like to be around, personally, to show you the watch. So, I'll mail it to you, and when the postman delivers it, don't open the package.

AL

Well, if I can't open the package, Matt . . . you might as well not send it at all. You can wear it, and show it to me when you come to Cleveland.

NEFFER

That sounds like a lot of trouble, Al.

BOB

Eighteen seconds to go, sir!

NEFFER

Say! (*Quickly*) I'd like to talk to your little boy, Al. I'd like to say hello to him.

AL

Sure. He's right here. Ronnie . . . say hello to your Uncle Matt!

NEFFER

Ronnie?

RONNIE

Hello, Uncle Matt. Know what I learned today?

NEFFER

No . . .

BOB

Seven seconds to go, sir!

NEFFER

What did you learn today, Ronnie?

RONNIE

I learned to hang up the phone, Uncle Matt!
                    (*Sound of phone hang up and buzz tone on line*)

NEFFER

Hello? Hello, Ronnie?

BOB

I'm sorry, Matt. You missed by one second!

NEFFER

Can you beat that?

BOB

But you're not going away empty-handed, sir. We've got some
wonderful prizes for you. First . . . a brand new chrome muffler for
your car from Ralph's of Hollywood . . . a back-scrubber brush
from the Upstate Boar Bristle Products Company . . . and a box of
waxed fruit from the Waxed Fruit Institute! It's all yours, Matt
Neffer, for playing *Phone Call to Anywhere*!

NEFFER

Thanks!

Salesman of the Year Award

BOB

We take you now to the grand ballroom of the Hotel Frimmler where the next voice you hear will be that of the President and Chief of Operations of the Wickwire Corporation, Mr. Carlton E. Wickwire.

WICKWIRE

(*Stentorian*) We're all here . . . to honor the man who . . . in my opinion . . . certainly deserves the title Salesman of the Year.
(*Applause*)

WICKWIRE

Come in here, Bill Jester. . . . Bill Jester is more than just a man. He's a salesman. And as such, he's entitled to the very best. I know that there are those among you who would say that Bill is more than a man . . . and a salesman. They would say he's a great human being, too.
(*More applause*)

WICKWIRE

Moreover, he's a man who never shirks his responsibilities . . . but looks them squarely in the eye. And I want you to know, Bill Jester, that you're aces with me. And right now, for selling eighteen percent over quota . . . and for the real pro you are . . . I want you to have this watch. Take it.

JESTER

Is it made of gold?

WICKWIRE

Why don't you unwrap the box and find out? I think you'll be pleasantly surprised.

JESTER

All right, I will. I'll look.

WICKWIRE

Well, Bill Jester . . . is it made out of gold?

JESTER

No, I don't think so. And what's more . . . it's not even running.

WICKWIRE

Let me look at it. Say, it isn't running at that, is it?

JESTER

No. It looks to me like the stem was put in crooked. Why don't you try banging it on something. They start up that way sometimes . . .

WICKWIRE

No, I'd rather have you do that. I don't want to be responsible.

JESTER

All right.

(*He slams it on podium and it flies apart,
spraying the watch insides all over.*)

WICKWIRE

Well, it certainly did fly apart, didn't it?

JESTER

Now that it's all apart, I can see a picture in the back of the case. It looks like somebody's mother. This isn't a new watch, is it?

WICKWIRE

Doesn't look like it, does it?

JESTER

Well, what do we do now? Do I get a new gift to replace the old watch?

WICKWIRE

I don't think so, Bill. You always were kind of careless with equipment!

JESTER

You know what? I hope your award ceremony melts in the hot sun.

WICKWIRE

(*Laughs*) Oh, come on, Bill Jester. We were only kidding. Couldn't you tell we were havin' a little fun with you?

JESTER

Yeah . . . I guess I could . . . ha ha . . .

WICKWIRE

You know we like to kid around once in a while.

JESTER

That's right, I forgot. I feel better.

WICKWIRE

What we really want you to have, Bill Jester is this . . .
(*Produces a scroll and signals for applause*)

JESTER

What is it?

WICKWIRE

It's a parchment scroll, Bill . . . hand-lettered, and suitable for framing. Here . . . let me read it! (*Reads from scroll*) "Bill Jester. He is more than just a man. He's a salesman. And, as such, he's entitled to the very best. There are those who would say he is more than a man . . . and a salesman . . . he's a —

JESTER

Hey, wait a minute!

WICKWIRE

Yes, Bill?

JESTER

You know what I hope?

WICKWIRE

What, Bill?

JESTER

I hope your scroll melts in the hot sun, too!

BULLETIN

BOB

We have been asked by the management to make the following announcement:

RAY

If anyone has seen a canoe drifting on the lake with red and white trim, and the name "Petunia" on it, and Mrs. Harrison B. Ogilvie *in* it, please notify Mr. Harrison B. Ogilvie at Wildwood Cottage, 346 Ring 2.

Monongahela Metal Foundry

BOB

Now a word to you ladies: Ladies, we don't expect you to take our word that Monongahela steel ingots are brighter and shinier than old-fashioned brands. Make a simple comparison test for yourself.

RAY

Just drag one of your present ingots out in the yard on a sunny day and place it next to one of ours. If the Monongahela ingot doesn't shine more brightly—even without hours of polishing—your money will be cheerfully refunded.

BOB

And here's important news of the sale of the year at your Monongahela Metal Foundry showroom.

RAY

Perhaps you're one of the many who's postponed buying new extra shiny steel ingots for your home because you thought you couldn't afford a full set of six. Well, now you need delay no longer, friends.

BOB

For a limited time only, your local Monongahela dealer is offering one ingot absolutely free with the purchase of any five at the regular price. So why not decorate your home for all the big holiday weekends that'll be coming up during the year ahead?

RAY

Visit your Monongahela agent and ask about his big six-for-the-price-of-five sale today!

Captain Pediatrician

RAY

Time now for another tale of adventure starring Captain Pediatrician—a mild-mannered family man by night who becomes a daring treater of children's disorders by day. As our story begins, young Sanford Bogash is just being ushered into the futuristic office of . . . Captain Pediatrician.

CAPTAIN

Well, hello there, Sanford. I understand from one of my informants that you haven't been feeling up to par the past few days.

SANFORD

Golly, Captain Pediatrician. That's true. But I can't imagine how you found out. You must have informants in strategic places all over. Either that or my mom told you I was sick when she called to make the appointment.

CAPTAIN

Don't concern yourself with how I found out, Sanford. Let's just say that waging eternal war against germs has led me to make some friends in very high places.

SANFORD

Gee whillikers, Captain Pediatrician! Does that mean you may even possess the strange power to cure my sniffles? Mom's already tried chicken soup and hot lemonade. But when neither of those things helped my sinus drainage, she said this was a job for Captain Pediatrician.

CAPTAIN

Well, I don't officially claim that I can work miracles, Sanford. But I will write out this prescription for you.

SANFORD

Gloryosky, Captain Pediatrician. Never before have my young eyes beheld such strange secret markings on a piece of paper. Will I be cured, once I eat it?

CAPTAIN

No. I don't want you to eat the paper, lad. I want you to take it to a pharmacy. There, the druggist will follow the coded message I've written, and give you an antibiotic to kill your germs.

SANFORD

Great day in the morning, Captain Pediatrician! An antibiotic racing through my little system to spread death among evil germs. You are indeed a worker of great medical wonders.

CAPTAIN

Thank you, Sanford. I like to think so.

RAY

And so—inside the young body of Sanford Bogash—another triumph of good over evil is destined to take place—thanks to the amazing powers of . . . Captain Pediatrician.

Pylomar

BOB

Just before we went on the air today, I met a gentleman in our studio audience who claims that he has one of the most fascinating stories of all time to tell. So I've invited him to come up here on stage. But I don't believe I caught your name, sir.

RUPPNICKER

I'm Emil Ruppnicker and I'm from Ponca City, Oklahoma.

BOB

Well, it's nice to have you with us. Now, about—

RUPPNICKER

That's kind of an interesting name, don't you think? Ruppnicker.

BOB

No. Not particularly. It just sounds German or something.

RUPPNICKER

Yes. It's of German derivation. Actually, my ancestors came from Württemberg, which was later absorbed into Germany.

BOB

I see. Well, if we can move along now—

RUPPNICKER

Well, aren't you going to ask me how it's spelled?

BOB

How what is spelled? Württemberg?

RUPPNICKER

No. Ruppnicker.

BOB

Well, I hadn't planned to. We don't usually waste time asking guests to spell their names.

RUPPNICKER

Well, in my case, I think you'd better.

BOB

Well, if it'll put you more at ease, I guess there's no harm in it.

RUPPNICKER

Okay. It's spelled P-Y-L-O-M-A-R.

BOB

I see. Well, now, if we can get to your story—

RUPPNICKER

Well, doesn't it strike you as being a little strange that Ruppnicker would be spelled P-Y-L-O-M-A-R?

BOB

No. Not particularly. Now this story of yours—

RUPPNICKER

Well, it strikes other people as strange. For example, I travel a lot in my work selling used razor blades on the road. And whenever I hit a new town, I always look up P-Y-L-O-M-A-R in the phone book and then call to ask if Mr. Ruppnicker is in. And do you know what the people who answer always tell me?

BOB

I wouldn't have the faintest.

RUPPNICKER

They tell me I have the wrong number. Here they've been going around for years with a name spelled P-Y-L-O-M-A-R and they don't even know it's pronounced Ruppnicker.

BOB

Yeah. Well, the literacy rate in your part of the country has never been too good. Now—

RUPPNICKER

Several years ago, I hired a chiropodist to try to trace the name back. But he couldn't do me any good.

BOB

Well, I'm not surprised. A chiropodist is a foot doctor.

RUPPNICKER

Yeah. I found that out after I'd already paid him his retainer.

BOB

Look, Mr. Ruppnicker, if we could just stop talking about your name and get around to your story.

RUPPNICKER

Well, that is my story. I have a name that isn't spelled anything like the way it's pronounced.

BOB

And that's what you had the gall to tell me was one of the most fascinating stories of all time?

RUPPNICKER

Sure. And I think this interview has been terribly interesting so far.

BOB

Well, when you use the term "so far," you imply that there is going to be more of it. And that's where you are mistaken. Now get out.

RUPPNICKER

Well, okay. But if you're ever in Ponca City, give me a ring. I'm in the book. The name is spelled—

BOB

I know how it's spelled.

RUPPNICKER

Well, at least I put that point across then. Good-bye.
(*Footsteps and door closing*)

BULLETIN

BOB

We have been asked by the management to make the following announcement: If anyone has seen a canoe drifting in the lake with red and white trim and the name "Petunia" on it, and Mrs. Harrison B. Ogilvie and a Mr. J. Watson Hammersmith in it, please notify Mr. Harrison B. Ogilvie at Wildwood Cottage, 346 Ring 2.

You and Your Income Tax

BOB

Welcome to *You and Your Income Tax,* featuring one of the nation's top experts in the field—the former assistant cashier of the Merchant's, Mechanics, Planters and Seaman's State Bank of Hibbing, Minnesota—Mr. Claude Flabbert. I had hoped to tell a bit about your background, Claude, but when I checked with the state board of certified public accountants they said they had never heard of you.

FLABBERT

Well, the reason the board has me listed under another name, Mr. Elliott, is that, for tax purposes, I maintain two separate identities. That way, it's possible for me to file a joint return with myself.

BOB

I imagine you could save quite a bit by doing that—especially since there is only one of you to feed and clothe.

FLABBERT

That's right. In fact, the idea has worked out so well that I'm creating several other people this year that the two of me can write off as exemptions.

BOB

And I suppose if you create enough dependents, you may not have to pay any tax at all.

FLABBERT

Well, actually, I could even show a profit by having my new people collect unemployment compensation, which is not taxable. That's the advantage of having your dependents be mythical adults rather than actual children.

BOB

Well, I'm sure your scheme will give our audience something to think about . . . but now I'd like to move along to a specific tax question sent in by one listener. He's from Rhode Island. "Dear Mr. Flabbert: During 1984, I held up the First National Bank of Prairie View, South Dakota . . . and escaped with eighty-two hundred dollars. I know I'll have to pay tax on this money, but can I deduct the cost of the getaway car as a business expense? Signed, Gerard W. Tibble." Oh . . . and in the P.S. he says, "Please don't mention my name on the air."

FLABBERT

Well you certainly can deduct the cost of maintaining a getaway car as a business expense. The only trouble is that you indicated you pulled only one robbery in 1984. This means that you can claim the deduction only from the time of the robbery—when you went on the lam—until the end of the year.

BOB

All right. Here's one from Springfield, New Jersey. "My fourteen-year-old son made twelve thousand dollars from his paper route in 1984 and my six-year-old daughter netted almost eight thousand dollars from the lemonade stand she operated in front of our house last summer. Can I claim them as exemptions anyway? Signed, Flabbergasted."

FLABBERT

No, you can't claim them as exemptions, but there is a chance that they may be able to claim you ... assuming you quit your own job and let them support you. In that case, you are their dependent.

BOB

I'm sure you made another household happier, Mr. Flabbert. Here's one from a Long Island listener that reads: "Last April, I changed my business from a privately owned venture to a corporation. I amortized the mortgage on my store building at the time, but I understand I can deduct the interest paid prior to April on my personal income tax. Would you please advise?"

FLABBERT

No, I certainly would not.

BOB

Well, why not, Mr. Flabbert?

FLABBERT

In the first place it's a silly question and in the second place, whoever wrote that letter sounds like one of those people who are always hunting for loopholes in the law. Next question?

BOB

But if he has a legitimate deduction ...

FLABBERT

I certainly won't help anyone trying to defraud the government. I'd advise this man to pay up and stop complaining. And I wish you wouldn't read mail like that on the air. It gives the feature a bad name.

BOB

All right. . . . Here's one from Red Bank, New Jersey. "I embezzled money last year from the place where I work, and bet it on the horses. I came out fifteen thousand dollars ahead. I replaced the money I stole and no one was the wiser. Do you think I should pay taxes on my track winnings?" The letter is signed "Fiscal."

FLABBERT

Let's not be foolish about this. If nobody knows you stole the money and nobody knows you bet on the horses, why in the world would you pay taxes on your winnings? My advice would be don't even file a return.

BOB

Well, I see our time is just about up for today, and let me thank you, Mr. Claude Flabbert, for giving us the benefit of your knowledge on . . . *You and Your Income Tax.*

FLABBERT

It was a pleasure, Bob . . . and will you see that the check for my appearance here is made out to cash?

BOB

I'll take care of it.

The Question Man

RAY

You know, we've had a lot of experts on our show today giving advice on all sorts of specialities, from medicine, investments, and consumer affairs to personal problems, vacations, and even coping with that old income tax, thanks to the knowledgeable Mr. Flabbert here.

BOB

Shrewd as they all are, though, none of them can match our next guest, and that's why we saved him for the end. You're in for a treat as the Jarwood Corporation—the nation's leading manufacturer of artificial police dogs—invites you to spend an informative session with Wilmont Shriber, the question man.

SHRIBER

To this very day, Ohio remains the only state in the union where Benjamin Harrison was born.

BOB

Just a moment, Wilmont. I haven't quite finished introducing you yet.

SHRIBER

No. The American League race has never finished with all ten teams tying for the pennant, even though such an occurrence is not specifically prohibited by the Commissioner.

BOB

I see. Well, if you could just hold on for half a minute there—

SHRIBER

Yes. The name selected for the War of 1812 did prove to be a mistake. This became obvious when all of the major battles were fought in 1814.

BOB

Well, that's very interesting but—

SHRIBER

No. Contrary to popular belief, the N.R.A. is still in existence. Now, however, the initials stand for the Nebraska Roofers' Association.

BOB

Wilmont, if you'll just control yourself, our first question today comes from a woman in Alaska.

SHRIBER

The United States did not acquire Alaska until 1867. Thus, there is no possible way it could have participated in the Civil War on either side.

BOB

Well, I imagine this woman already knows that. Her question is: "Do we see lightning before we hear the accompanying thunder because light travels faster than sound—or is it just the opposite?"

SHRIBER

Is this on standard or daylight time that she wants the thing explained?

BOB

Well, she doesn't say—but I'm sure it doesn't have any bearing on the question.

SHRIBER

No. You're mistaken about that. On daylight time, our clocks are advanced—so she'd hear the thunder almost an hour before she saw the lightning.

BOB

Wilmont, the relative speed of light and sound has nothing to do with what time it is.

SHRIBER

Well, it's bound to. When we go on daylight time, we just make it get dark an hour later. We don't monkey around with the normal schedule of when we hear things at all.

BOB

Well, in any event, you're avoiding the question.

SHRIBER

No. I'm merely avoiding the answer. It's the woman who's avoiding the question. So what do we have next there?

BOB

Well, I have a card here from a man in Peru, Indiana.

SHRIBER

Peru is in South America.

BOB

He writes—

SHRIBER

I say, Peru is in South America.

BOB

Well, this man thinks he's in Indiana, and he writes: "How could Washington have thrown a silver dollar across the Potomac when there weren't any silver dollars at the time he was supposed to have done it?"

SHRIBER

This is the Potomac he's asking about specifically?

BOB

That's right.

SHRIBER

Well, it's ridiculous to ask about coinage dates and then single out one particular river when the U.S. Mint wasn't even set up on that basis. So what's next?

BOB

Finally, there's a letter here from a woman in Oregon who asks: "At the time of his first inauguration, wasn't Theodore Roosevelt younger than President Kennedy?"

SHRIBER

Well, let's see. Theodore Roosevelt was inaugurated sixteen years before Mr. Kennedy was born. So you subtract that and . . . no, wait. You take eight and six ... I mean ten and six.... When Theodore Roosevelt was forty-four ...

(*Pause*)

And so, on behalf of my sponsor and crew, this is Wilmont Shriber, thanking you for your attention, and saying ... so long for now!

Tippy, the Wonder Dog

(*Theme. Establish and fade for*)

BOB

And now Mushies—the great cereal that gets soggy even without milk or cream—brings you another exciting story of adventure starring Tippy, the Wonder Dog.
(*Dog bark*)

BOB

As we look in on the isolated cabin of Grandpa Witherspoon today, we find that floodwaters are raging through the valley. Gramps has climbed to the very peak of the roof—and is clinging desperately to the chimney. Meanwhile, little Jasper stands nearby, looking out at the muddy river. Suddenly, he turns and speaks . . .

JASPER

The water's still rising, Gramps.

GRAMPS

Consarn it all! I know the water's still rising. And that fool dog of yours we sent for help will never get through. He's probably up in one of those trees right now—just sitting it out.

JASPER

Oh, Tippy never quits when I send him out on a vital mission, Gramps. He's the bravest, smartest dog in the whole wide world.

GRAMPS

Well, consarn it all! We sent him out with a note tied around his neck when the water was only ankle-deep. That was a week ago.

JASPER

Don't worry, Gramps. I know you can't swim—and you wouldn't last two minutes in that raging water. But Tippy'll save you. He's the finest, smartest dog in the whole wide world.

GRAMPS

Well, consarn it all! Where is he?

JASPER

Ahoy! I think I see him now. I'll make my way down to the edge of the roof and help him up here.
(*Scraping across shingles. Then splash.*)

JASPER

Here Tippy, Tippy, Tippy!
(*Scraping across shingles*)

GRAMPS

Consarn it all! He didn't even swim over this way.

JASPER

That wasn't Tippy after all, Gramps. it was just the Logans' terrier swimming home from the Red Cross with more blood plasma.

GRAMPS

Consarn it all! Every other dog in the neighborhood can go on a simple errand in an emergency. But that fool Tippy's just got himself lost someplace.

JASPER

He's not lost, Gramps. But you specified in the note you tied around his neck that you wanted to be rescued by a helicopter. And Tippy may have had to swim clear out to the airport to find one. But he'll make it. He's the greatest, smartest— Wait! here he comes now. I'll give him a hand.
(*Scraping across shingles. Then splash.*)

JASPER

Here Tippy, Tippy, Tippy!
(*Scraping across shingles*)

GRAMPS

Consarn it all! He swam right by.

JASPER

Yeah. But it wasn't Tippy. It was that new puppy they've got up at the Osmer place. He was swimming home with some typhoid serum.

GRAMPS

Consarn it all! That pup can't be more than a month old. And he's already doing errands we could never train Tippy to do.

JASPER

Don't say that, Gramps. Tippy's the grandest, smartest dog in the whole wide world. And look over there! He's coming for sure now. I'll help him up here.
(*Sliding on shingles. Then splash.*)

JASPER

That's it, Tippy. Shake yourself off good. Fine old dog.
(*Sliding on shingles*)

GRAMPS

Well, consarn it all. The dog's back—but where's the helicopter?

JASPER

Just a minute. Tippy's got a different note around his neck. It's from the helicopter pilot. And listen to what it says: "Your dog bit me, so I threw him out of the plane."

GRAMPS

Consarn it all! If we come out of this alive, that dog's going straight to the pound.

JASPER

But don't you understand, Gramps? Tippy wouldn't have gotten that excited if he hadn't heard the engine misfiring. And I'll bet he was just trying to make the pilot throw him out so he could swim home and let us know the plane wasn't safe. Didn't I tell you? He's the brightest, smartest dog in the whole wide world.
(*Theme. Establish and fade for*)

BOB

Today's thrilling story has been brought to you by Mushies—the great new cereal that gets soggy even without milk or cream. Join us again soon for more exciting adventures of . . . Tippy, the Wonder Dog.

(*Theme up briefly and then out*)

Election Editorial

BOB

At this time, we wish to direct an important Bob and Ray public affairs editorial to those who will be voting in next Thursday's special election.

RAY

Of course, that includes all of you in the 95th and 96th wards— the precincts beyond there that adjoin the railroad track—the easternmost corner of the 73rd aldermanic district—and the whole unincorporated area south of that.

BOB

As well as the entire village of Twixby, if there are any registered voters left there.

RAY

Exactly. And throughout that district, our Bob and Ray experts strongly urge you to vote "No" on Proposition J. We consider it a poorly written piece of legislation that may even be unconstitutional.

BOB

Very true. For example, paragraph 5 of the proposition would permit over-the-counter sales—but only to those who can prove that they are at least eighteen years old—or are accompanied by an adult.

RAY

We think this provision is unenforceable. For one thing, they can't be sold over the counter because they are too heavy to lift over the counter. But the smart alecks in the state capital didn't even consider that.

BOB

Even worse, the restriction of sales to those over eighteen is an infringement on the rights of law-abiding citizens who may be only eleven or twelve.

RAY

Right. And as we all know, the largest share of the market for these items is the under-eighteen group—especially over-the-counter. So for this reason alone, we would urge a "No" vote on Tuesday.

BOB

However, we've spoken of only part of the tragedy that Proposition J would create. In addition, Paragraph 6 would require a minimum deposit of ten cents on each container at the time of purchase.

RAY

Notice if you will that no mention is made of a maximum deposit. That ten cents is only a minimum. And you know what a field day the politicians would have with a loophole like that.

BOB

Our experts estimate that the deposit on glass jars, which are the most popular containers for this item, would double within a year. The increase might be even larger on brands that come in earthenware pots or Styrofoam humidors.

RAY

Undoubtedly. And it raises the question of why you and I and other working people should spend our good money just to prevent the littering of old jars and pots. We already have people on the public payroll who are responsible for picking up that stuff. And Proposition J certainly doesn't mention firing those goldbricks.

BOB

No. That's another obvious boondoggle in the making. But we think that the wording of Paragraph 8 is even worse. It provides that no sales could be made in establishments where food is also served—or where household pets are not kept on a leash.

RAY

Frankly, we're at a loss to explain why only household pets are covered by this paragraph. We don't think the voters want animals of any kind running loose in establishments where food is served.

BOB

Of course, we've already heard what the bureaucrats have to say about that. They claim that Proposition J deals only with over-the-counter sales and a minimum deposit on containers. But if that's the case, why mention household pets at all?

RAY

Why indeed? Also, it should be noted that Proposition J never defines the term "household pets." Presumably, dogs and cats would be included. But what about horses and camels? That's a question that could be kicking around in the courts for years.

BOB

In a similar vein, this proposition doesn't define the type of leash it proposes for domestic animals. Must it be made of leather—or can we simply tie a loose rope or even a short length of piano wire around the neck of our pet?

RAY

Surely, no voter would want his small animal restrained with piano wire. But the political hacks in the capital don't seem to care.

BOB

We could go on and on about the evils of Proposition J. For example, there is no mention of fluoridation—even though it's vital to the health of children under eighteen, who already are being excluded.

RAY

From making over-the-counter purchases, you mean.

BOB

Exactly. It's all there in the fine print—which makes us wonder where the money came from to put this proposition on the ballot in the first place.

RAY

We all know that political clout doesn't come cheap. And the very fact that Proposition J discriminates against those under eighteen, as well as household pets and dental hygienists, should tell us something. We'd be willing to bet that this proposal is being pushed by out-of-state interests.

BOB

Frankly, we don't think that the voters will prove to be as dumb as they look. And we're counting on a strong "No" vote to bury this issue once and for all.

RAY

Don't let corrupt bureaucrats and out-of-state millionaires tell you how to vote.

BOB

You have been listening to an editorial opinion expressed by the Bob and Ray Public Affairs Department. This editorial does not necessarily represent the views of our employees and members of their families. We encourage responses from qualified persons who have opposing opinions.

RAY

True. Of course, in this case, we're positive that no one who has an opposing opinion could possibly be a qualified person. So please don't bother to ask for equal time.

BOB

Yes. Especially for not bothering us—thank you.

Voting Booths

RAY

Speaking of elections—ever wonder what becomes of voting booths between elections? They must go someplace . . . but where? To check out the matter, we sent ace reporter Wally Ballou to Winona, Minnesota—where he forwards this story . . .

BALLOU

—ly Ballou at the National Voting Booth Storage Company, Winona, Minnesota, with the manager on duty, Mr. Walter Kettlehut. As I understand it, sir, you're not the owner of the firm . . .

KETTLEHUT

No, I'm just more or less a watchman, you might say. After all, once the booths all get here after an election, there isn't too much to do but keep an eye on them.

BALLOU

And all of the booths are here now from the last election, I presume?

KETTLEHUT

Well . . . we still have a few outlying precincts to hear from . . . but almost all of them are here now.

BALLOU

And quite a sight they make! They're stored outdoors, and stretch in all directions as far as the eye can see. How many acres of them are here, Mr. Kettlehut?

KETTLEHUT

Around four thousand acres now, Mr. Ballou. Of course, with the population growing so rapidly, there are more precincts in each election; consequently more booths.

BALLOU

So your firm has to keep buying additional land to store them?

KETTLEHUT

Right. We have to add about a hundred acres a year. And we figure by 1996, there'll be no agriculture carried on in this county at
all.

BALLOU

The whole thing will be filled up with voting booths. Certainly is
an amazing prospect.

KETTLEHUT

It is amazing. Now, back in the 1890s, when the firm was first or-
ganized, the booths were kept indoors in a warehouse. But, after
Utah, Arizona and New Mexico were admitted to the Union, it
all got out of hand.

BALLOU

And you've been storing the booths outdoors ever since.

KETTLEHUT

Couldn't find a building anyplace big enough to hold them all.

BALLOU

Now, I know you have very severe winters here in Minnesota.
Doesn't it damage the booths . . . being out in the weather?

KETTLEHUT

Well, the little curtains you pull closed when you're voting
usually have to be replaced for each election. But the weather
doesn't seem to hurt the booths themselves.

BALLOU

It doesn't?

KETTLEHUT

I've seen a time when the booths were completely covered with snow. But, when spring came . . . there they were again.

BALLOU

I see.

KETTLEHUT

We did have a tornado once. Should have seen those booths flying all over the place. Boy! What a mess! Ha ha . . .

BALLOU

Guess that's the most exciting thing that's ever happened to you on your job here . . .

KETTLEHUT

No . . . I think the most exciting thing happened after the 1984 election. Some people in New Hampshire forgot to take the voting machines out of the booths before they sent them out here.

BALLOU

What did you do?

KETTLEHUT

We didn't do anything.

BALLOU

I see. Well that's the picture then and thanks for giving me this story, Mr. Kettlehut.

KETTLEHUT

My pleasure.

BALLOU

And this is Wally Ballou returning it to the studio.

RAY

. . . where all we have time to say is that takes us to the end of another broadcast day. So thanks for listening, everybody. This is Ray Goulding saying—excuse me? What was that?

BULLETIN

BOB

I was just going to say, Ray, that before we go we have one final bulletin for our listeners. We've been asked to make the following announcement: Found . . . drifting on the lake, one canoe, with red and white trim, the name "Petunia" on it, and shotgun holes above the waterline. Owner may obtain same by calling Joe's Boathouse.

RAY

I bet that's a load off someone's mind, Bob. And now this is Ray Goulding, saying . . . Write if you get work.

BOB

And Bob Elliott, reminding you to hang by your thumbs. Goodnight, folks.

RAY

Goodnight.

Bob and Ray's next public appearance will be at the South Sewauket, Rhode Island, Firehouse on Friday and Saturday evenings.

Gents:	$1.50
Ladies:	1.00
One Gent and One Lady Together:	$2.00
One Gent and Two Ladies:	5.00
Three Gents and One lady:	6.50
Two Ladies Together:	7.50

Neckties Required.

Index